Step by Step Exchange 2013 On-Premise to 365 – Hybrid Migration

Chetan Pawar

Bachelor's in Computers (**B.E.**)
MCSA, MCSE, MCTS, MCITP in
Windows 2000, 2003, 2008, 2012, Exchange 2003, 2007, 2010, 2013
Windows XP, 7 and 8 Clients, VMWare, Hyper-, 365, Azure and Cloud Computing
CompTIA, HP and Dell Certified Technician
Microsoft Certified Trainer (**MCT**) since August 2004 and Author of various books.

ISBN:1539037770
ISBN-13:9781539037774

Contents

ACKNOWLEDGMENTS

Shree Swami Smartha

To my parents for educating me so well so I can proudly say that I am use-less
To my wife who has always been besides me in thick and thin
To all those who write and share their IT experiences free online
Finally, to all those of you who inspire me when you buy a copy - thanks

ON PREMISES READINESS AND OFFICE 365 ACCOUNT CREATION

Readiness:

We will start the Hybrid configuration with Readiness which is an assessment phase of the current customer environment.

- What is your current on-premises Exchange environment?
1. Exchange Server 2013
2. Exchange Server 2010
3. Exchange Server 2007
- Do you want all users to use their on-premises credentials (Single Sign on) when they log on to their Exchange Online mailbox?

Yes or No

- How do you want to route inbound Internet mail for both your on-premises and Exchange Online mailboxes?
✓ Route all inbound Internet mail for both organizations through Exchange Online Protection

OR

✓ Route all inbound Internet mail for both organizations through my on-premises Exchange servers
- Do you want mail sent between your Exchange Online and on-premises organizations to go through an Edge Transport server?

Yes or No

- Make sure following ports are open.

Transport Protocol	Upper Level Protocol	Feature /Component	On-premises Endpoint	On-premises Path	Authentication Provider	Authorization Method	Pre-Auth Supported?
TCP 25 (SMTP)	SMTP/TLS	Mail flow between Office 365 and on-premises	Exchange 2013 CAS/EDGE Exchange 2010 HUB/ EDGE	N/A	N/A	Certificate-based	No

TCP 443 (HTTPS)	Auto disco ver	Autodis cover	Excha nge 2013/ 2010 CAS	/autodiscover/au todiscover.svc/w ssecurity /autodiscover/au todiscover.svc	Azure AD authe nticat ion syste m	WS-Secur ity Authe nticat ion	No
TCP 443 (HTTPS)	EWS	Free/bu sy, MailTips , Messag e Tracking	Excha nge 2013/ 2010 CAS	/ews/exchange.a smx/wssecurity	Azure AD authe nticat ion syste m	WS-Secur ity Authe nticat ion	No
TCP 443 (HTTPS)	EWS	Multi-mailbox search	Excha nge 2013/ 2010 CAS	/ews/exchange.a smx/wssecurity /autodiscover/au todiscover.svc/w ssecurity /autodiscover/au todiscover.svc	Auth Serve r	WS-Secur ity Authe nticat ion	No
TCP 443 (HTTPS)	EWS	Mailbox migratio ns	Excha nge 2013/ 2010 CAS	/ews/mrsproxy.s vc	Basic	Basic	No
TCP 443 (HTTPS)	Auto disco ver EWS	OAuth	Excha nge 2013/ 2010 CAS	/ews/exchange.a smx/wssecurity /autodiscover/au todiscover.svc/w ssecurity /autodiscover/au todiscover.svc	Auth Serve r	WS-Secur ity Authe nticat ion	No

TCP 443 (HTTPS)	N/A	AD FS	WIN2008/2012 Server	/adfs/*		Azure AD authentication system	Varies per config.	2-factor

Concept And Prerequisite:

The concept and prerequisite is important to understand so added this for the blog followers so that it can clear any confusion. These are the definition of these technical terms which are good to understand in Microsoft wordings so please read on TechNet.

We would suggest *searching* for the Exchange Server Deployment Assistant and going through it to the end as it gives you an excellent idea of how ready things practically are.

AND

Also *search* for MS KB jj200581 and thoroughly read it especially with the goal of understanding the terminology, process and options before you follow steps in this book.

Microsoft Exchange Online Protection service (EOP) is included in all Office 365 for enterprises tenants by default and works with on-premises Exchange 2013 Client Access servers to provide secure message delivery between the on-premises and Exchange Online organizations. Depending on how your organization is configured, it may also handle routing incoming mail from external recipients for your Exchange Online organization and your on-premises Exchange organization.

Hybrid Configuration wizard: Exchange 2013 includes the Hybrid Configuration wizard which provides you with a streamlined process to configure a hybrid deployment between on-premises Exchange and Exchange Online organizations.

Windows Azure AD authentication system and ADFS: The Windows Azure AD authentication system is a free cloud-based service that acts as the trust broker between your on-premises Exchange 2013 organization and the Exchange Online organization. On-premises organizations configuring a hybrid deployment must have a federation trust with the Windows Azure AD authentication system. The federation trust can either be created manually as part of configuring federated sharing features between an on-premises Exchange organization and other federated Exchange organizations or as part of configuring a hybrid deployment with the Hybrid Configuration wizard. A federation trust with the Windows Azure AD authentication system for your Office 365 tenant is automatically configured when you activate your Office 365 service account.

Active Directory synchronization Active Directory synchronization replicates on-premises Active Directory information for mail-enabled objects to the Office 365 organization to support the unified global address list (GAL). Organizations configuring a hybrid deployment must deploy Active Directory synchronization on a separate, on-premises server.

Supported organizations: Active Directory synchronization between the on-premises and Office 365 organizations is a requirement for configuring a hybrid deployment. All customers of Azure Active Directory and Office 365 have a default object limit of 300,000 objects (users, mail-enabled contacts, and groups) by default. At the same time if you have more objects contact Azure Admin to increase the quota.

Hybrid deployment management: You manage a hybrid deployment in Exchange 2013 via a single unified management console that allows for managing both your on-premises and Office 365 Exchange Online organizations. The *Exchange admin center* (EAC), which replaces the Exchange Management Console and the Exchange Control Panel, allows you to connect and configure features for both organizations. When you run the Hybrid Configuration wizard for the first time, you will be prompted to connect to your Exchange Online organization. You must use an Office 365 account that is a member of the Organization Management role group to connect the EAC to your Exchange Online organization.

Certificates: Secure Sockets Layer (SSL) digital certificates play a significant role in configuring a hybrid deployment. They help to secure communications between the on-premises hybrid server and the Exchange Online organization. Certificates are a requirement to configure several types of services. If you're already using digital certificates in your Exchange organization, you may have to modify the certificates to include additional domains or purchase additional certificates from a trusted certificate authority (CA). If you aren't already using certificates, you will need to purchase one or more certificates from a trusted CA.

Bandwidth: Your network connection to the Internet will directly impact the communication performance between your on-premises organization and the Exchange Online organization. This is particularly true when moving mailboxes from your on-premises Exchange 2013 server to the Exchange Online organization. The amount of available network bandwidth, in combination with mailbox size and the number of mailboxes moved in parallel, will result in varied times to complete mailbox moves. Additionally, other Office 365 cloud-based services may also affect the available bandwidth for messaging services. Before moving mailboxes to the Exchange Online organization, you should:

- Determine the average mailbox size for mailboxes that will be moved to the Exchange Online organization.
- Determine the average connection and throughput speed for your connection to the Internet from your on-premises organization.
- Calculate the average expected transfer speed, and plan your mailbox moves accordingly.

Unified Messaging: Unified Messaging (UM) is supported in a hybrid deployment between your on-premises and Exchange Online organizations. Your on-premises telephony solution must be able to communicate with the Exchange Online organization. This may require that you purchase additional hardware and software. If you want to move mailboxes from your on-premises organization to the Exchange Online organization, and those mailboxes are configured for UM, you should configure UM in your hybrid deployment prior to moving those mailboxes. If you move mailboxes before you configure UM in your hybrid deployment, those mailboxes will no longer have access to UM functionality which you would not want.

Information Rights Management: Information Rights Management (IRM) enables users to apply Active Directory Rights Management Services (AD RMS) templates to messages that they send. AD RMS templates can help prevent information leakage by allowing users to control who can open a rights-protected message, and what they can do with that message after it's been opened. IRM in a hybrid deployment requires planning, manual configuration of the Exchange Online organization, and an understanding of how clients use AD RMS servers depending on whether their mailbox is in the on-premises or Exchange Online organization.

Mobile devices: Mobile devices are supported in a hybrid deployment. If Exchange ActiveSync is already enabled on Client Access servers, they'll continue to redirect requests from mobile devices to mailboxes located on the on-premises Mailbox server. For mobile devices connecting to existing mailboxes that are moved from the on-premises organization to Exchange Online, the Exchange ActiveSync partnership must be disabled and re-established before redirection requests are processed correctly. All mobile devices that support Exchange ActiveSync should be compatible with a hybrid deployment.

Client requirements: Recommended clients use Outlook 2013 or Outlook 2010 for the best experience and performance in the hybrid deployment. Pre-Outlook 2010 clients have limited support in hybrid deployments and with the Office 365 service so they are not preferred clients.

Licensing for Office 365: To create mailboxes in, or move mailboxes to, an Exchange Online organization, you need to sign up for Office 365 for enterprises and you must have licenses available. When you sign up for Office 365, you'll receive a specific number of licenses that you can assign to new mailboxes or mailboxes moved from the on-premises organization. Each mailbox in the Exchange Online service must have a license.

Antivirus and anti-spam services: Mailboxes moved to the Exchange Online organization are automatically provided with antivirus and anti-spam protection by Microsoft Exchange Online Protection (EOP). You may need to purchase additional EOP licenses for your on-premises users if you chose to route all incoming Internet mail through the EOP service. Carefully evaluate whether the EOP protection in your Exchange Online organization is also appropriate to meet the antivirus and anti-spam needs of your on-premises organization. If you have protection in place for your on-premises organization, you may need to upgrade or configure your on-premises antivirus and anti-spam solutions for maximum protection across your organization.

Public folders: Public folders are now supported in Office 365, and on-premises public folders can be migrated to Exchange Online. Additionally, public folders on Exchange Online can be moved to the on-premises Exchange 2013 organization. Both on-premises and Exchange Online users can access public folders located in either organization using Outlook Web App, Outlook 2013, Outlook 2010 SP2 or Outlook 2007 SP3. Existing on-premises public folder configuration and access for on-premises mailboxes doesn't change when you configure a hybrid deployment.

A typical onsite Exchange 2013 Deployment
This diagram on the next page is courtesy Microsoft and I have simply copied it. All server names are informative only.

Current Client connectivity Architecture

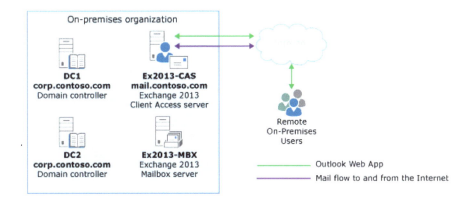

Future Hybrid Architecture: Once you will configure the Hybrid Exchange with your on Premise and office 365, it will look like below image.

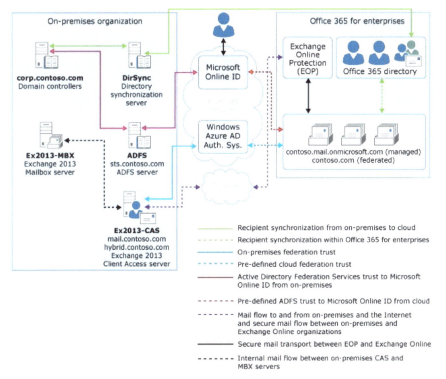

Office 365: Register a domain Register a domain. **Make sure to do not change the DNS records until we reach to a cut over point**.

Verify Office 365 account version:

- Hybrid deployments are supported in all Office 365 plans that support Windows Azure Active Directory synchronization.
- All Office 365 Enterprise, Government, Academic and Midsize plans support hybrid deployments.
- Office 365 Small Business and Home plans **don't support hybrid deployments**. so it is important to verify that if your plan is ready to support hybrid deployment. Make sure, your Office 365 plan is one of the supported plans.
- Your Office 365 tenant must also be version 15.0.000.0 or higher for the hybrid deployment to function correctly with Exchange 2013.
- To verify the version and status of your existing Office 365 tenant, do the following:
- Connect to the Office 365 tenant using remote Windows PowerShell.

```
PS C:\WINDOWS\system32> $Cred = Get-credential
cmdlet Get-Credential at command pipeline position 1
Supply values for the following parameters:
Credential
PS C:\WINDOWS\system32> $Session = New-PSSession -ConfigurationName Microsoft.Exchange -ConnectionUri https://ps.outlook
.com/powershell/ -Credential $Cred -Authentication Basic -AllowRedirection
WARNING: Your connection has been redirected to the following URI:
"https://pod51044psh.outlook.com/powershell-liveid?PSVersion=4.0"
PS C:\WINDOWS\system32> Get-Executionpolicy
RemoteSigned
PS C:\WINDOWS\system32> Import-PSSession $Session
WARNING: The names of some imported commands from the module 'tmp_s4k5jr1v.blg' include unapproved verbs that might
make them less discoverable. To find the commands with unapproved verbs, run the Import-Module command again with the
Verbose parameter. For a list of approved verbs, type Get-Verb.

ModuleType Version    Name                             ExportedCommands
---------- -------    ----                             ----------------
Script     1.0        tmp_s4k5jr1v.blg                 {Add-AvailabilityAddressSpace, Add-DistributionGroupMember...
```

- After connecting to the Office 365 tenant, run the following command.

Get-OrganizationConfig | FLAdminDisplayVersion,IsUpgradingOrganization

Verify that your Office 365 tenant and status meet the following requirements:
   ✓ *AdminDisplayVersion* parameter value is greater than 15.0.000.0
   ✓ *IsUpgradingOrganization* parameter value is False

For example, "0.20 (15.1.118.22)" and "False".

```
PS C:\WINDOWS\system32> Get-OrganizationConfig | Fl AdminDisplayVersion,IsUpgradingOrganization

AdminDisplayVersion      : 0.20 (15.1.118.22)
IsUpgradingOrganization : False
```

- Disconnect from the Office 365 tenant remote PowerShell session. Run the below command.

Remove-PSSession $Session

ADFS Server requirement: At least one ADFS server should be there to sync mail-enabled active directory objects. This will be called Active Directory Synchronization Server.

Exchange server requirement:

- Exchange 2013 servers configured in a hybrid deployment must have one of the following operating systems installed:

- ✓ 64-bit edition of Windows Server 2008 R2 Datacenter RTM or later
- ✓ 64-bit edition of Windows Server 2008 R2 Standard Service Pack 1
- ✓ 64-bit edition of Windows Server 2008 R2 Enterprise Service Pack 1
- ✓ 64-bit edition of Windows Server 2012 Standard or Datacenter

- Exchange 2013 servers configured with the Client Access and Mailbox server roles.
- All on-premises Exchange 2013 servers must have installed Cumulative Update 1 (CU1) or greater for Exchange 2013 to support hybrid functionality with Office 365.

On Premise Active Directory: In the Active Directory site where your existing Exchange 2010 servers are deployed, you must have at least one writeable domain controller running any of the following:
- ✓ Windows Server 2003 Standard Edition with SP1 or later (32-bit or 64-bit)
- ✓ Windows Server 2003 Enterprise Edition with SP1 or later (32-bit or 64-bit)
- ✓ Windows Server 2008 Standard or Enterprise RTM or later (32-bit or 64-bit)
- ✓ Windows Server 2008 R2 Standard or Enterprise RTM or later
- ✓ Windows Server 2008 Datacenter RTM or later
- ✓ Windows Server 2008 R2 Datacenter RTM or later
- ✓ Windows Server 2012 Standard or Datacenter

Additionally, the Active Directory forest must be Windows Server 2003 forest functional level or higher.

SETTING UP THE ADFS AND SSO – SINGLE SIGN ON

Before we start the single sign on process we need to gather the information which will be used in configuring Hybrid between Exchange on premise and office 365. You can make the following table to gather information about your existing organization that you're going to need before you get started.

Description	Example value in checklist	Value in your organization
Active Directory forest root	chetanpawar.com	
Internal Exchange 2013 server host name (contains Mailbox and Client Access server roles)	cpmail13	
External Exchange 2013 server FQDN	mail.chetanpawar.com	
Primary SMTP namespace	chetanpawar.com	
User principal name domain Microsoft Online ID domain	chetanpawar365.com	

The following table lists new services that you configure as part of the hybrid deployment. Replace chetanpawar.com with your domain name for the values you provide in the table.

Description	Example value in checklist	Value in your organization
Internal Active Directory Federation Services (AD FS) server hostname (only for organizations choosing to deploy single sign-on)	cpadfs	
External AD FS server FQDN (only for organizations choosing to	sts.cpadfs.com	

deploy single sign-on)

Internal Active Directory synchronization server host name	CPDC1
On-premises Autodiscover FQDN	autodiscover.chetanpawar.com
Service tenant FQDN **Note** You can only choose the subdomain portion of this FQDN. The domain portion must be "onmicrosoft.com".	chetanpawar365.onmicrosoft.com

Configure Single sign-on

Single sign-on enables users to access both the on-premises and Office 365 tenant service organizations with a single user name and password. Configuring single sign-on also allows you to enforce your organization's password policies and account restrictions in both the on-premises and Office 365 tenant service organizations.

Follow the below steps to configure single sign-on for your on-premises organization:

> **Prerequisites** Add additional physical or virtual servers to your on-premises organization to support an installation of Active Directory Federation Services (AD FS), and make sure the servers meet the requirements to run AD FS.

➢ Have Active Directory deployed and running in either Windows Server 2003 R2, Windows Server 2008, Windows Server 2008 R2, Windows Server 2012, or Windows Server 2012 R2 with a functional level of mixed or native mode.

➢ If you plan to use AD FS as your STS, you will need to do one of the following:

➢ Download, install and deploy AD FS 2.0 on a Windows Server 2008 or Windows Server 2008 R2 server. Also, if users will be connecting from outside your company's network, you must deploy an AD FS 2.0 proxy.

➢ Install the AD FS role service on a Windows Server 2012 or Windows Server 2012 R2 server.

➢ If you plan to use Shibboleth Identity Provider as your STS, you will

> need to install and prepare an operational Shibboleth Identity Provider.

> ➢ Based on the type of STS you will set up, use the Microsoft Azure Active Directory Module for Windows PowerShell to establish a federated trust between your on-premises STS and Azure AD.

> ➢ Install the required updates for your Microsoft cloud service subscriptions to ensure that your users are running the latest updates of either Windows 7, Windows Vista, or Windows XP. Some features may not work properly without the appropriate versions of operating systems, browsers, and software.

Prepare AD:

Active Directory must have certain settings configured in order to work properly with single sign-on. In particular, the user principal name (UPN), also known as a user logon name, must be set up in a specific way for each user. To prepare your Active Directory environment for single sign-on, we recommend that you run the Microsoft Deployment Readiness Tool. This tool inspects your Active Directory environment and provides a report that includes information about whether or not you are ready to set up single sign-on. If not, it lists the changes you need to make to prepare for single sign-on. For example, it inspects whether or not your users have UPNs and if those UPNs are in the correct format.

Depending on each of your domains, you may need to do the following:

> ➢ The UPN must be set and known by the user.
> ➢ The UPN domain suffix must be under the domain that you choose to set up for single sign-on.
> ➢ The domain you choose to federate must be registered as a public domain with a domain registrar or within your own public DNS servers.
> ➢ To create UPNs, follow the instructions in the Active Directory topic Add User Principal Name Suffixes. Keep in mind that UPNs that are used for single sign-on can only contain letters, numbers, periods, dashes, and underscores.
> ➢ If your Active Directory domain name is not a public Internet domain (for example, it ends with a ".local" suffix), you must set a UPN to have a domain suffix that is under a Internet domain name that can be registered publically. We recommend that you use something familiar to your users, such as their email domain.
> ➢ If you have already set up Active Directory synchronization, the user's UPN may not match the user's on-premises UPN defined in Active Directory. To fix this, rename the user's UPN using the Set-MsolUserPrincipalName cmdlet in the Microsoft Azure Active Directory Module for Windows PowerShell.

All in All please fix the issues highlighted in this readiness check.

Plan the Directory Sync Method: For sure you would like to go for single sign on so this is the time to decide and select the appropriate single sign-on deployment topology. Let us see what are the option here.

Azure AD: Extending your on-premises directories to Azure AD provides the following benefits:

➢ Simplifying your cloud-based administrative tasks
➢ Providing your users with a more streamlined sign-in experience
➢ Obtaining single sign-on to all cloud-based applications
➢ Securely and seamlessly managing your user and device identities, both cloud and on-premises, through a unified experience
➢ Managing your first- and third-party applications, SaaS and other existing enterprise cloud and on-premises applications through a unified experience
➢ Azure AD supported scenarios:
➢ Directory synchronization: Once directory sync has been set up, administrators can manage directory objects from your on-premises Active Directory and those changes will be synchronized to your tenant. In this scenario, your **users will use different user name and passwords to access your cloud and on-premises resources**.
➢ **DirSync with Password Sync** – MS KB dn441214 - Used when you want to enable your users to sign in to Azure AD and other services using the same user name and password as they use to log onto your corporate network and resources. Password sync is a feature of the Directory Sync tool. But this is not single sign-on. It means you will used the same user id and password but you will have to login multiple times.
➢ **DirSync with Single Sign-On** – MS KB dn441213 - Used to provide users with the most seamless authentication experience as they access Microsoft cloud services while logged on to the corporate network. In order to set up single sign-on, organizations need to deploy a security token service on-premises, such as Active Directory Federation Services (AD FS). Once it has been set up, users can use their Active Directory corporate credentials (user name and password) to access the services in the cloud and their existing on-premises resources. ADFS is the key component here which allows us to configure Single sign-on.
➢ **Multi-forest – DirSync with Single Sign-On** – MS KB dn441214 - Used to provide users with the most seamless authentication experience as they access Microsoft cloud services while logged on to the corporate network. In order to set up single sign-on, organizations need to deploy Active Directory Federation Services (AD FS) as security token service on-premises. Once it has been set up, users can use their Active Directory corporate credentials (user name and password) to access the services in the cloud and their existing on-premises resources. This is the 4th scenario

where you are using multiple forest.

Directory Synchronization tools: There are 3 tools available to provide directory sync for hybrid setup.

➢ DirySync – Azure Active Directory Synchronization Tool
➢ AAD Sync – Azure Active Directory Synchronization Services
➢ FIM – Forefront Identity Manager 2010 R2

Azure Active Directory Connect Microsoft has released the AAD connect tool on June 18th 2015. AAD Connect streamlines the experience of extending your local directories into Azure AD so that fewer tools are required to install; it guides you through the entire experience so you are not required to read many pages of documentation; and it reduces the on-premises footprint because you are not required to deploy many servers. AAD Connect is a single wizard that performs all of the steps you would otherwise have to do manually for connecting your Windows Server Active Directory to Azure Active Directory:

➢ It downloads and installs prerequisites like the .NET Framework, Azure Active Directory PowerShell Module, and Microsoft Online Services Sign-In Assistant
➢ It downloads, installs and configures Dirsync (or AAD Sync), and enables it in your Azure AD directory.
➢ It configures either the password sync or the single sign-on scenario, depending on which sign-on option you prefer, including any required configuration in Azure.
➢ It checks to make sure that your configuration is working!

Install and Configure: This is the most critical step where we need to configure single sign-on between your on-premises organization and Office 365 tenant service. Let us see in the following steps

The best way to configure ADFS is to follow the check list mentioned in the in Microsoft KB Article jj205462.

ADFS Terminology

AD FS term	Definition
AD FS configuration database	A database used to store all configuration data that represents a single AD FS instance or Federation Service. This configuration data can be stored using the Windows Internal Database (WID) feature included with Windows Server 2008, Windows Server 2008 R2, and Windows Server 2012 or using a Microsoft SQL Server database.
Claim	A statement that one subject makes about itself or another subject. For example, the statement can be about a name,

	email, group, privilege, or capability. Claims have a provider that issues them (in this case a Microsoft cloud service customer) and they are given one or more values. They are also defined by a claim value type and, possibly, associated metadata.
Federation Service	A logical instance of AD FS. A Federation Service can be deployed as a standalone federation server or as a load-balanced federation server farm. The name of the Federation Service defaults to the subject name of the SSL certificate. The DNS name of the Federation Service must be used in the Subject name of the Secure Sockets Layer (SSL) certificate.
Federation server	A computer running Windows Server 2008, Windows Server 2008 R2, or Windows Server 2012 that has been configured to act in the federation server role for AD FS. A federation server serves as part of a Federation Service that can issue, manage, and validate requests for security tokens and identity management. Security tokens consist of a collection of claims, such as a user's name or role.
Federation server farm	Two or more federation servers in the same network that are configured to act as one Federation Service instance.
Federation server proxy	A computer running Windows Server 2008, Windows Server 2008 R2, or Windows Server 2012 that has been configured to act as an intermediary proxy service between a client on the Internet and a Federation Service that is located behind a firewall on a corporate network. In order to allow remote access to the cloud service, such as from a smart phone, home computer, or Internet kiosk, you need to deploy a federation server proxy.
Web Application Proxy	In Active Directory Federation Services in Windows Server 2012 R2, the role of a federation server proxy is handled by a new Remote Access role service called Web Application Proxy. To enable your AD FS for accessibility from outside of the corporate network (in other words, to configure extranet access), which is the purpose of deploying a federation server proxy in legacy versions of AD FS (AD FS 2.0 and AD FS in Windows Server 2012), you can deploy one or more Web

	Application Proxies for AD FS in Windows Server 2012 R2. For more information about the Web Application Proxy, see KB dn280944.
Relying party	A Federation Service or application that consumes claims in a particular transaction.
Relying party trust	In the AD FS Management snap-in, a relying party trust is a trust object that is created to maintain the relationship with another Federation Service, application, or service (in this case the Microsoft Azure Active Directory (Microsoft Azure AD) service) that consumes claims from your organization's Federation Service.
Network load balancer	A dedicated application (such as Network Load Balancing) or hardware device (such as a multilayer switch) used to provide fault tolerance, high availability, and load balancing across multiple nodes. For AD FS, the cluster DNS name that you create using this NLB must match the Federation Service name that you specified when you deployed your first federation server in your farm.

You need to updated ADFS with an Update Rollup 2 for Active Directory Federation Services (AD FS) 2.0 if you are using Windows 2008 R2 server and this available for download as Microsoft KB 2681584.

There is no hotfix need and thus not available for windows 2012.

Certificate: This SSL certificate must contain the following with private key:
Subject name and subject alternative name must contain your federation service name, such as fs.domain.com.
Subject alternative name must contain the
value **enterpriseregistration** followed by the UPN suffix of your organization, such as, for example,**enterpriseregistration.domain.com**
I am using wildcard cert so it should be fine.
The token-signing certificate must contain a private key, and it should chain to a trusted root in the Federation Service. By default, AD FS creates a self-signed certificate. However, depending on the needs of your organization, you can change this later to a CA-issued certificate by using the AD FS Management snap-in.

Recommendation: Use the self-signed token-signing certificate generated by AD FS. By doing so, AD FS will manage this certificate for you by default. For example, in case this certificate is expiring, AD FS will generate a new self-signed certificate to use ahead of time.
Have a look on the certificate requirement as per Microsoft KB Article dn1513311.

DNS record: Create a host record for fs.domain.com for the ADFS server.
Create a CName record **enterpriseregistration** pointing to fs.domain.com. A CNAME record is required in order to enable name resolution for the Device Registration Service (DRS)

Service Account: Create a service account which will be required while configuring ADFS to continuously sync directories.
I have created **ADFS2SVC** account and checked "password never expires". Add this user to the domain admins of the AD domain.

Configure ADFS: This is the time to ensure ADFS is configured and working file
- Install the AD FS software on the computers that will become federation servers by running the following command:
- *Install-windowsfeature adfs-federation -IncludeManagementTools*
- Configure the AD FS software on one of the computers to act in the federation server role.
- On the Server Manager **Dashboard** page, click the **Notifications** flag, and then click **Configure the federation service on the server**.

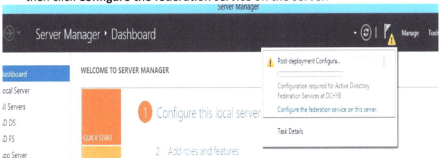

- The **Active Directory Federation Service Configuration Wizard** is launched.
- On the **Welcome** page, select **Create the first federation server in a federation server farm** and click **Next**.

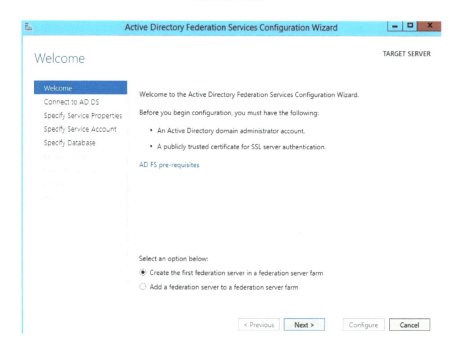

- On the **Connect to AD DS** page, specify the service account which we had created earlier then click **Next**.

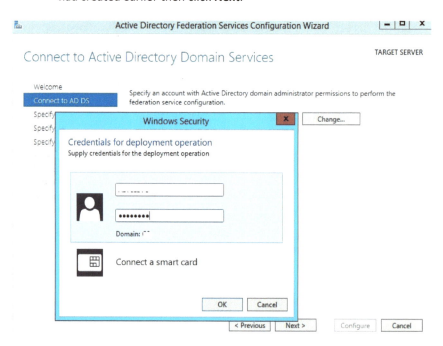

- On the **Specify Service Properties** page, do the following and then click **Next**:
  - ➢ Import the .pfx certificate file or select from dropdown.
  - ➢ Provide a name for your federation service. For example, **fs.domain.com**. This name must match one of the subject or subject alternative names in the certificate.
  - ➢ Provide a display name for your federation service. For example, **Domain Corporation**. This name will be shown to users at the AD FS sign-in page.

- On the **Specify Service Account** page, specify a service account. You can either create or use an existing group Managed Service Account (gMSA) or use an existing domain user account.

The benefit of using a gMSA is its auto-negotiated password update feature. If you want to use a gMSA, you must have at least one domain controller in your environment that is running Windows Server 2012 operating system.

If the gMSA option is disabled and you see an error message similar to **Group Managed Service Accounts are not available because the KDS Root Key has not been set**, you can enable gMSA in your domain by executing the following Windows PowerShell command on a Windows Server 2012 or later domain controller in your Active Directory domain:

Add-KdsRootKey –EffectiveTime (Get-Date).AddHours(-10)

```
Windows PowerShell
Copyright (C) 2014 Microsoft Corporation. All rights reserved.

PS C:\Users\PN> Add-KdsRootKey -EffectiveTime (Get-Date).AddHours(-10)

Guid
----
4d69c0f4-ade3-7e38-f774-cd865af3f03d


PS C:\Users\PN> _
```

Then return to the wizard and click the **Previous** button followed by the **Next** button to re-enter the **Specify Service Account** page. The gMSA should now be enabled, and you can select it and enter a desired gMSA account name. I am using my service account.

- On the **Specify Configuration Database** page, specify an AD FS configuration database and then click **Next**. You can either create a database on this computer using Windows Internal Database (WID) or you can specify the location and the instance name of the SQL server.

- Now **Review Options** and click **Next**.

- On the **Pre-requisite Checks** page, verify that all pre-requisite checks were successfully completed, and then click **Configure**.

- On the **Results** page, review the results and whether the configuration has completed successfully, Click **Close** to exit the wizard.

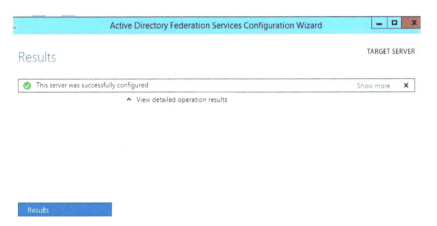

- Try to browse the following URLS to test the working of ADFS
https://fs.domain.com/federationmetadata/2007-06/federationmetadata.xml

HmmPsUXIegh+TvEfdGgFiKSR4xzaMzmLEFKdWHIXDyE=V0EVdxgDhCnCDFs7H3Kp69Z3eLI
AddressThe e-mail address of the userGiven NameThe given name of the userNameThe unique name
name of the userAD FS 1.x E-Mail AddressThe e-mail address of the user when interoperating with A
UPN of the user when interoperating with AD FS 1.1 or AD FS 1.0RoleA role that the user hasSurnam
identifier of the userAuthentication time stampUsed to display the time and date that the user was auth

https://fs.domain.com/adfs/ls/idpinitiatedsignon.htm - here you can see the name is being used

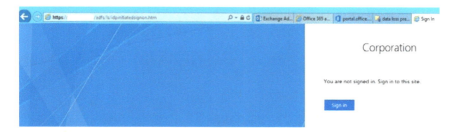

Add fs.domain.com in local intranet

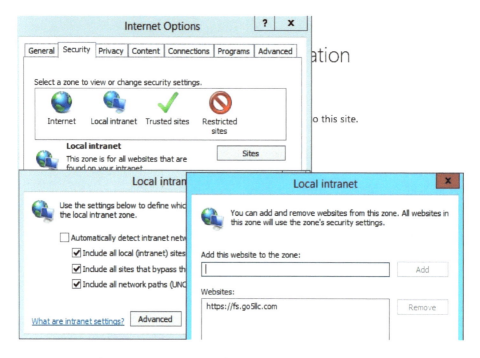

- Open the AD FS Management from Server manager

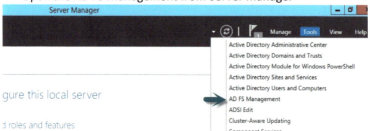

- ADFS mmc will look like as shown below:

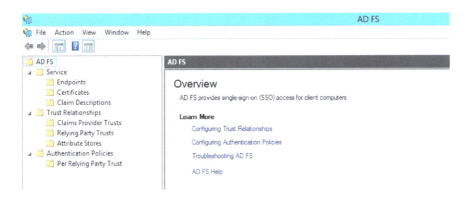

Add another node in the ADFS farm. You can add another node by installing ADFS on another server.

Add a Web Proxy. The Web Application Proxy can provide access to web applications from extranet clients using AD FS claims-based authentication or Windows Integrated Authentication. The Web Application Proxy can be used in conjunction with Active Directory workplace join, multifactor authentication, or multifactor access control in order to enable more flexible and manageable resource access by users and devices outside of a company firewall.

- **Enabling Device Registration Service**

To enable the Device Registration Service in the local forest, the following prerequisites must be met:

➢ The Active Directory schema must be at Windows Server® 2012 R2 level.

➢ You need to run Windows PowerShell cmdlets as a member of the Enterprise Admins group in order to enable DRS.

➢ The group managed service account that was specified for the AD FS configuration must be specified for the value of the – **ServiceAccountName** parameter in the format *domainaccount_name*.

➢ Run this command and give same user id which we just configured to update AD for device registration:

Initialize-ADDeviceRegistration –serviceaccountname domainsvc

```
PS C:\Users\PN> Initialize-ADDeviceRegistration
cmdlet Initialize-ADDeviceRegistration at command pipeline position 1
Supply values for the following parameters:
ServiceAccountName: g5\ADFS2SVC

This command will prepare Active Directory to host Device Registration Service in the current forest.
Do you want to continue with this operation?
[Y] Yes  [A] Yes to All  [N] No  [L] No to All  [S] Suspend  [?] Help (default is "Y"): Y
WARNING: The Active Directory forest has been prepared for Device Registration.  To use the AD FS Device Registration
Service, run the Enable-AdfsDeviceRegistration cmdlet on each node in your AD FS farm.

Message                        Context                        Status
-------                        -------                        ------
The configuration completed successf... DeploymentSucceeded            Success
```

Now the command to enable device registration.

Enable-AdfsDeviceRegistration

- On the ADFS1 server, in the **AD FS Management** console, navigate to **Authentication Policies**. Select **Edit Global Primary Authentication**. Select the check box next to **Enable Device Authentication**, and then click **Apply, OK**.

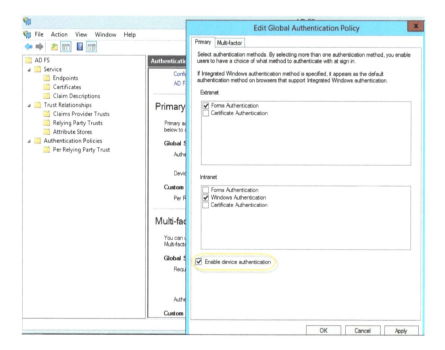

Configuring ADFS extranet access

We need to configure the proxy ADFS in DMZ to secure ADFS server. Please follow the Microsoft KB dn528859 for this.

Connect/Install Azure AD Powershell

- Go to google and search for Microsoft Online Services Sign-In Assistant for IT Professionals RTW.
- Download the **msoidcli** and install.

- Accept the agreement and click install

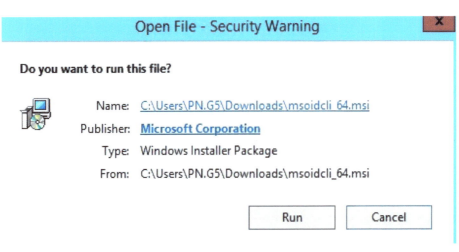

- Click on Finish once installed.
- Download the Azure AD by searching for "**azure active directory module for windows PowerShell**" and then start the installation as an

administrator.

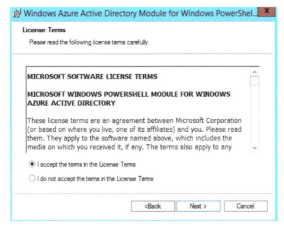

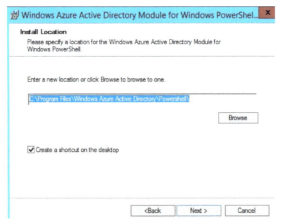

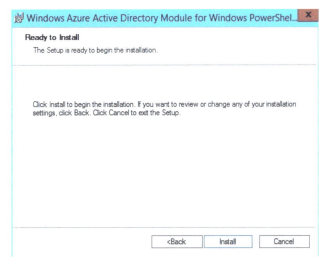

Click on finish once done.

- **Connect to Azure AD**

Open Azure AD from the desktop Icon

Run the following command to connect to Azure AD

$msolcred = get-credential
connect-msolservice -credential $msolcred

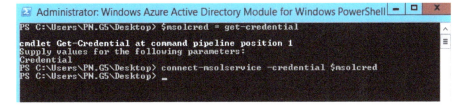

Run the following commands to download help

new-item c:MSOLHelp -type directory
get-command | Where-Object {$_.name -like "*msol*"} | format-list | Out-

File c:MSOLHelpmsolcmdlets.txt
  notepad c:MSOLHelpmsolcmdlets.txt

Run the command to verify your user
  Get-Msoluser

Set up a trust between AD FS and Azure AD

This is one of the crucial steps. Let us see the steps. Each domain that you want to federate must either be added as a single sign-on domain or converted to be a single sign-on domain from a standard domain. Adding or converting a domain sets up a trust between AD FS and Microsoft Azure Active Directory (Microsoft Azure AD).

Continue on the same Azure AD PowerShell.

Run the following command to add a federation

Run New-MsolFederatedDomain –DomainName <domain>, where <domain> is the domain to be added and enabled for single sign-on.

In our case we will convert so we have to run the following command

Run Convert-MsolDomainToFederated –DomainName <domain>, where <domain> is the domain to be converted. This cmdlet changes the domain from standard authentication to single sign-on.

```
PS C:\Users\PN.G5\Desktop> Convert-MsolDomainToFederated -DomainName      .com
Successfully updated 'Go5llc.com' domain.
PS C:\Users\PN.G5\Desktop> _
```

To verify that the conversion has worked, compare the settings on the AD FS server and in Azure AD by running

Get-MsolFederationProperty –DomainName <domain>. If they don't match, you can run Update-MsolFederatedDomain –DomainName <domain> to sync the settings.

My domain got this

```
PS C:\Users\PN.G5\Desktop> Get-MsolFederationProperty -DomainName      .com

Source                        : ADFS Server
ActiveClientSignInUrl         : https://fs.      .com/adfs/services/trust/200
                                5/usernamemixed
FederationServiceDisplayName  : Go5LLC Corp
FederationServiceIdentifier   : http://fs.go5llc.com/adfs/services/trust
FederationMetadataUrl         : https://fs.go5llc.com/adfs/services/trust/mex
PassiveClientSignInUrl        : https://fs.go5llc.com/adfs/ls/
PassiveClientSignOutUrl       : https://fs.go5llc.com/adfs/ls/
TokenSigningCertificate       : [Subject]
                                  CN=ADFS Signing - fs.Go5llc.com

                                [Issuer]
                                  CN=ADFS Signing - fs.Go5llc.com

                                [Serial Number]
                                  6A24F       797BF

                                [Not Before]
                                  6/17/2015 11:25:38 AM

                                [Not After]
                                  6/16/2016 11:25:38 AM

                                [Thumbprint]
                                  43E94       7
```

```
NextTokenSigningCertificate     :
PreferredAuthenticationProtocol :

Source                          : Microsoft Office 365
ActiveClientSignInUrl           : https://fs.       .com/adfs/services/trust/200
                                  5/usernamemixed
FederationServiceDisplayName     : Golden Five Global
FederationServiceIdentifier      : http://fs.       .com/adfs/services/trust
FederationMetadataUrl            : https://fs.       .com/adfs/services/trust/mex
PassiveClientSignInUrl           : https://fs.       .com/adfs/ls/
PassiveClientSignOutUrl          : https://fs.       .com/adfs/ls/
TokenSigningCertificate          : [Subject]
                                     CN=ADFS Signing - fs.       .com

                                   [Issuer]
                                     CN=ADFS Signing - fs.       .com

                                   [Serial Number]
                                     6A24H                    BF

                                   [Not Before]
                                     6/17/2015 11:25:38 AM

                                   [Not After]
                                     6/16/2016 11:25:38 AM

                                   [Thumbprint]
                                     43E94                    ?7

NextTokenSigningCertificate     :
PreferredAuthenticationProtocol : WsFed
```

At the same time you will see "Possible Service issue" in the office 365 portal. This is because of the federation has updated and it might have broken the SPF record. I simply stopped checking DNS issue.

So I ran Update-MsolFederatedDomain –DomainName domainname because federated service displayname showing different and after the command it got fixed.

```
Source                          : Microsoft Office 365
ActiveClientSignInUrl           : https://fs.       .com/adfs/services/trust/2005
                                  /usernamemixed
FederationServiceDisplayName     :       Corp
FederationServiceIdentifier      : http://fs.       .com/adfs/services/trust
FederationMetadataUrl            : https://fs.       .com/adfs/services/trust/mex
PassiveClientSignInUrl           : https://fs.       .com/adfs/ls/
PassiveClientSignOutUrl          : https://fs.       .com/adfs/ls/
TokenSigningCertificate          : [Subject]
                                     CN=ADFS Signing - fs.       .com

                                   [Issuer]
                                     CN=ADFS Signing - fs.       .com
```

ACTIVE DIRECTORY SYNCHRONIZATION – Onsite >> Online

Directory Synchronization is important for us to do the smooth login and migration to office 365. We need to sync all the users and DLs with correct attributes. To review the AD objects Microsoft has provided the utility named Idfix to fix the AD attributes.
I would refer to MVP Benoit Hemat blog on Idfix.
Please follow this blog and fix your AD objects attributes as suggested.
Once IDs are fixed then only move to the next step.

Prerequisite: Let us have a look on prerequisite and make sure they are installed.

- AD Forest should be 2003 or higher
- Domain Controllers should be Windows 2003 SP1 or higher
- Dir Sync Computer must be domain joined.
- Dir Sync computer must be 64 bit with OS windows 2008 SP1 and above.
- Dir Sync computer must be running .net framework 3.5 SP1 and 4.5.1
- Dir Sync Computer must have PowerShell
- You can only install one computer running the Directory Sync tool between an on-premises Active Directory and an Office 365 tenant.
- You must be domain Admins, local admin of dirsync computer and admin in office 365.

The Azure AD service supports synchronization of up to 50,000 mail-enabled objects. To synchronize more than 50,000 mail-enabled objects, you must contact Microsoft Support.
Objects that have been synchronized from your on-premises directory service appear immediately in the Global Address List (GAL); however, these objects may take up to 24 hours to appear in the Offline Address Book (OAB) and in Skype for business Online.

Hardware Requirement: Depends on number of objects in the AD to sync.

Number of objects in Active Directory	CPU	Memory	Hard drive size
Fewer than 10,000	1.6 GHz	4 GB	70 GB
10,000–50,000	1.6 GHz	4 GB	70 GB
50,000–100,000 Requires full SQL Server	1.6 GHz	16 GB	100 GB
100,000–300,000 Requires full SQL Server	1.6 GHz	32 GB	300 GB
300,000–600,000 Requires full SQL Server	1.6 GHz	32 GB	450 GB
More than 600,000 Requires full SQL Server	1.6 GHz	32 GB	500 GB

Split Domain name:
Many organizations use different domain name for AD domain and email domain. To handle this issue we can update the UPN with the email domain as a fix.

1st method is update all users userprinciplename but alternative is adding alternate UPN in AD trust and forest.

Below are the steps to configure alternate UPN.

- Click **Start**, Administrative Tools, and then click **Active Directory Domains and Trusts**.
- Log on to one your organization's Active Directory domain controllers
- In the console tree, right-click **Active Directory Domains and Trusts** and then click **Properties**.
- Select the **UPN Suffixes** tab, type an alternative UPN suffix for the forest, and then click **Add**.
- Repeat step 3 to add additional alternative UPN suffixes

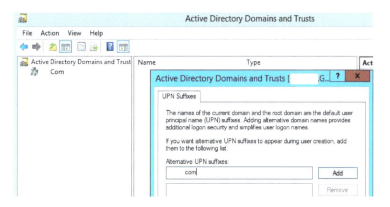

Now it will look like below:

Activate Directory Synchronization:

To activate directory synchronization, use the following steps:

- Install and run the [Microsoft Deployment Readiness Tool.](#) Try to fix the issues which are showing here.
- Depending on which portal you are using, do one of the following:
  - ➢ If you are using Office 365 or another account portal, click **Users**, click **Set up** next to **Active Directory synchronization**, and then proceed to the next step.
  - ➢ If you are using the Azure Management Portal, click **Active Directory**, click on your directory showing on the **Enterprise Directory** page, click **Directory Integration**, and then proceed to the next step.
  - ➢ If you are using the Azure AD Preview Portal, in the left pane, click **Integration**, click **Deploy directory sync**, and then proceed to the next step.
- Click **Activate**.

I am using first option.

I reached to this page and clicked on Activate in 3rd step.

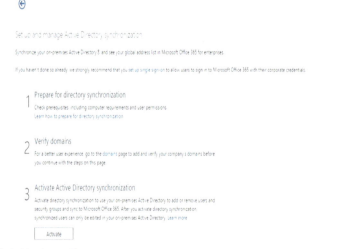

- Click Activate on the popup

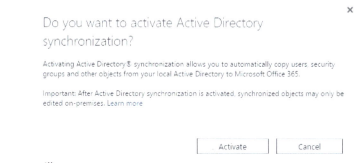

Now you will see

Active Directory synchronization is activated.

Install Dir Sync tool – At this time we are ready to install Dir Sync tool. We have 3 options available to use

1. **Dirsync.exe** – This is the default tool which is expected to be decommissioned sooner. This tool only support single AD forest.
2. **WAAD** – This tool allows multi forest directory sync and it was released in September 2014.
3. **Azure AD Connect tool** – Refer to page 24 of this document for details of this awesome tool.

Before we start the Azure AD Connect setup and wizard. Run the following on your ADFS server.

1. Login to the ADFS server.
2. Open **Windows PowerShell** with **Run As Administrator**.
3. Run the following command
4. Enable-PSRemoting –force

If you miss this step then you will see this error ...

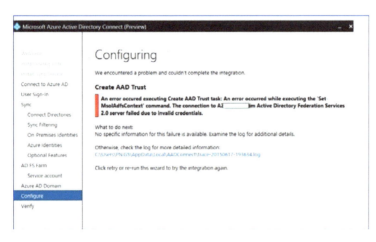

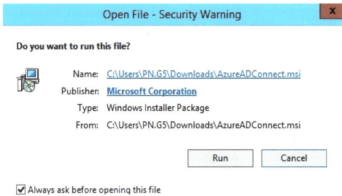

Click on run and it will install Azure AD connect.

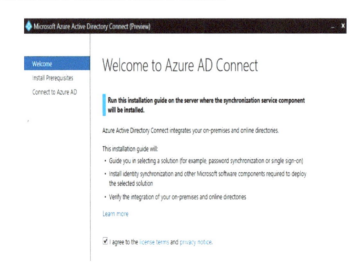

Now you will see the options which can be configured. Click install once ready.

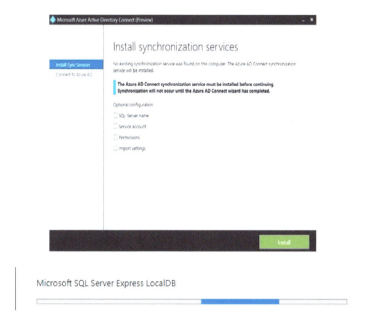

It will install Sql db where Metaverse will be stored.
Now it will install synchronization service.

Now Provide Azure AD credentials and click next.

It is recommended you create a service account in Azure AD. This id should be a member of Global Administrator group. We should also set password never expires.
Run the below command to enable "Password Never Expires"

Set-MsolUser -UserPrincipalName alias@domain.com -PasswordNeverExpires $true

Now this is the most interesting screen. Especially if you have multiple forest.

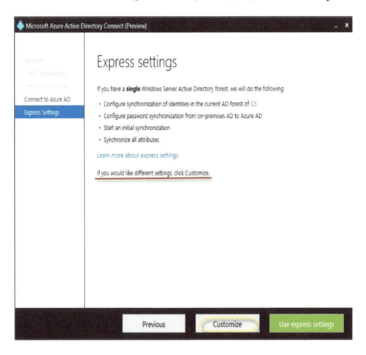

I don't prefer express setting so I click on customize, I see the below screen with 3 options and for single sign we should use Federation with ADFS.

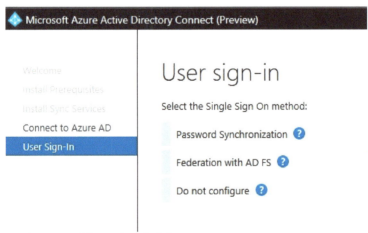

Select Federation with ADFS and click next.
Give the AD user id and passed to add this AD. Continues to add more AD.

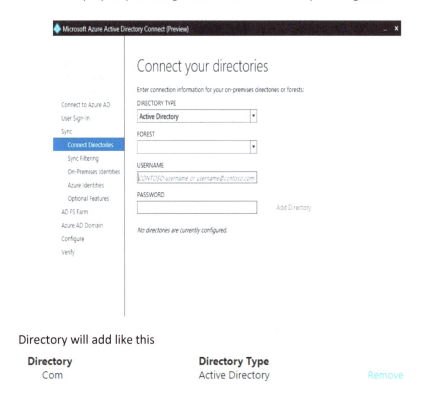

Directory will add like this

Directory   **Directory Type**
Com   Active Directory   Remove

Now we have an option to sync either all users + groups or select a group and only its members will be synced. Click next.

Select from the 2 options if the same user exist in multiple active directories or one. I have selected only one.

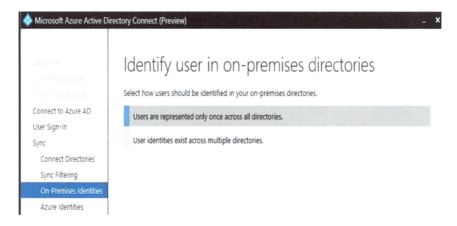

In a multi-forest you might select some other attributes but mostly we use default attributes.

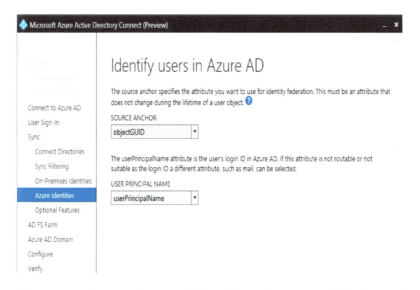

There are various options available. I have just selected "Exchange hybrid deployment".

If you are deploying Active Directory synchronization with your Exchange 2013 organization then you should select this option because **it grants the Windows Azure Active Directory Sync tool write access to your local Active Directory in support of hybrid deployment features specific to on-premises Exchange 2013 organizations**.

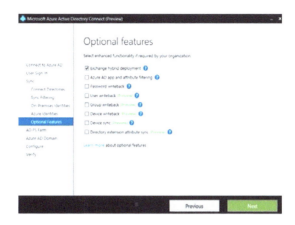

I have already created ADFS farm but if you have not created one, this wizard will create. Give the ADFS server name and click next.

Give the ADFS service id and password and click next

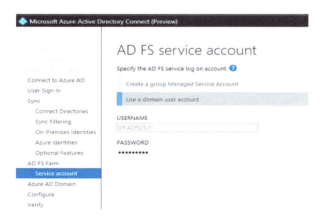

Select Azure AD domain and click next.

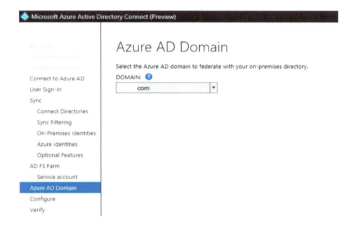

Here comes the summary of what it is going to run.

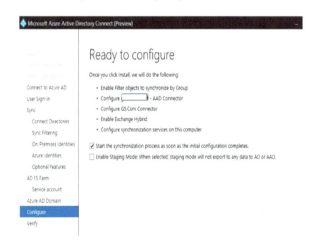

Now it will configure everything.

Installation Completed here.

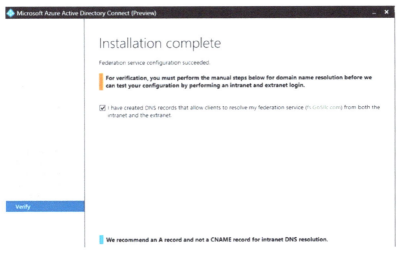

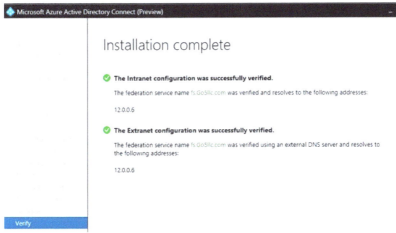

Exit from the setup.

DirSync Connectors configuration

Now we have configured the DIRSYNC. Time to configure the connectors in MetaVerse.

Open "**Synchronization Service Manager**" and Go to Connectors

Tab and Go to the properties of On Premise AD

Connector and Select **"Configure Directory Partitions"** and Click on

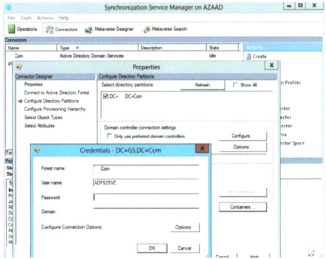

Containers.

Type the password and click ok. Then select the OUs and click ok then ok.

To avoid all sync I had configured staging which was preventing from syncing the AD objects to Azure AD.

If you had enabled staging earlier then it is the time to disable the staging mode so open AAD Connect and login. Then select **"Disable Staging Mode"** and click next

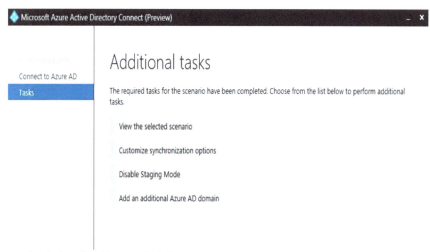

Uncheck the checkbox and click next

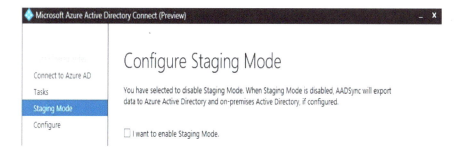

Click install on this screen

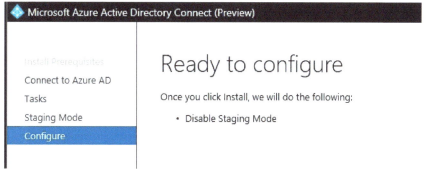

In few seconds you will see the below screen. Click exit.

By default, directory synchronization occurs once every three hours as it is configured in Task Scheduler.

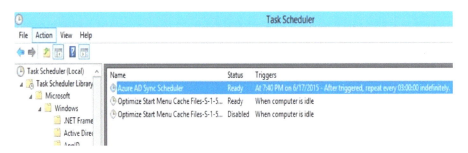

To force immediate directory synchronization, open a command prompt with elevated privileges and start the DirectorySyncClientCmd tool from C:Program FilesMicrosoft Azure AD SyncBin:

```
C:\Program Files\Microsoft Azure AD Sync\Bin>DirectorySyncClientCmd.exe
.Com
Initializing
Importing...
Synchronizing from all Sources..
Synchronizing from Target.
Exporting to Target....
Exporting to all Sources.
Finished
C:\Program Files\Microsoft Azure AD Sync\Bin>
```

Login to Office 365 and check the active users and you will see users synced their status will show "Synced with Active Directory"

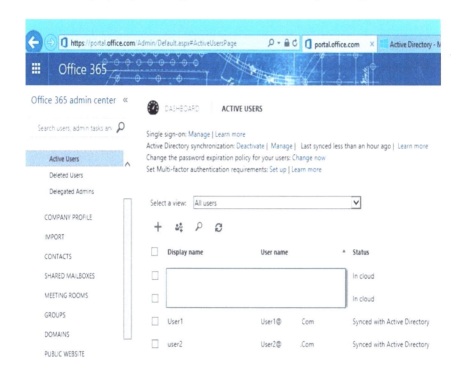

Same in Azure AD

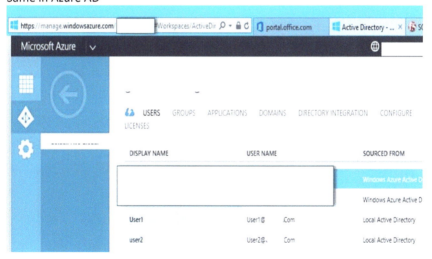

The question might come why only 2 users got synced when we have 3 in the Test OU which is the scope. Answer is group membership. So only member of the group will sync as we configured in the beginning.

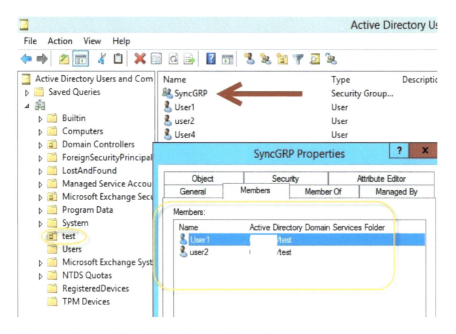

If you run into a DIRSYNC issue then try the tool at :–
https://configure.office.com/scenario.aspx?sid=18&uid=534f4349414c
This tool will run the following tests.

All results Issues

◢ Directory Synchronization: Checking whether synchronization is enabled

Looks like you're good to go. We've confirmed that Active Directory synchronization is activated.

◢ Directory Synchronization: Making sure that your Active Directory is synchronizing on schedule with Office 365

You're good to go. Your directory synchronized with Office 365 in the last three hours (Last DirSync Time in UTC - 6/18/2015 5:44:45 AM).

◢ Directory Synchronization: Checking if Directory Synchronization with password sync is running on your server

You're good to go. Directory Synchronization with password sync appears to be running in the 24 hours. Details from your server: 'Password Synchronization Manager has started.

G5.'

◢ Directory Synchronization: Checking if password synchronization has not informed Office 365 of a recent password change of one ore more of your users in the past 30 minutes

There was a synchronization of one of your user's passwords in the past 30 minutes. Details 'Provision credentials ping end. TrackingID : 5c2857f5-37e0-496e-9c87-3e72a3b25608.'

◢ **Azure AD Connect: Checking to see if the synchronization service is running**

You're good to go, the service is running.

Activate Synced User:

Select the user and on the extreme right corner click on "Activate synced users"

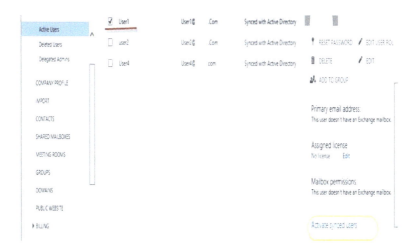

Assign the applications and click on activate to enable licenses.

Click on Finish here.

The ACTUAL stuff – HYBRID CONFIGURATION

Exchange 2013 Hybrid Configuration

DNS Changes:

➤ **Autodiscover Host Record:** To enable Outlook 2013, Outlook 2010, Outlook 2007, and mobile clients to connect to mailboxes in the Exchange Online organization, you need to configure an Autodiscover record on your public DNS. Autodiscover automatically configures client settings so that users don't need to know server names or other technical details to configure their mail profiles. This should be configure as autodiscover.domain.com pointing to your exchange 2013 CAS servers. I am expecting that this record is already configured and working. This is one of the innovation that Exchange 2013 will be able to recognize if the user is in exchange or office 365. SRV based Autodiscover redirect method is not supported for on-premises Exchange & Exchange Online federation.

➤ **SPF Txt Record:** Microsoft also recommend that you configure a Sender Policy Framework (SPF) record to ensure that destination email systems trust messages sent from your domain and the Exchange Online Protection (EOP) service for your Office 365 organization. The SPF record for your organization uses the Sender ID Framework. The Sender ID Framework is an email authentication protocol that helps prevent spoofing and phishing by verifying the domain name from which email messages are sent. Sender ID validates the origin of email messages by verifying the IP address of the sender against the alleged owner of the sending domain.

For SPF we have 3 options. First route all your emails via office 364, second route all your emails via exchange 2013 and third both to send emails out. Based on your configuration add the IP and hostname to the SPF txt record. You can add maximum of 10 entries in one record and you can have multiple records.

DNS records will look like below:

Hybrid requirement	DNS record	DNS record type	Target and value
Required for all hybrid deployments	autodiscover.contoso.com	CNAME or A	If using CNAME DNS: mail.contoso.com If using A DNS: External IP address of an Exchange 2013 Client Access server or firewall
Recommended as a best practice for all hybrid deployments	SPF	TXT	v=spf1 include:spf.protection.outlook.com ~all

Certificates: Digital certificates are an important requirement for secure communications between on-premises Exchange 2013 servers, clients, and the Exchange Online organization. You need to obtain a certificate that will be installed on Client Access and Edge Transport servers from a third-party trusted certificate authority (CA). Secure communications for internal connections between the on-premises Exchange 2013 Client Access and Mailbox servers use self-signed certificates. Microsoft recommends that your certificate's common name match the primary SMTP domain for your organization.

If you have separate CAS and MBX roles then you will have to import the certificate to the mailbox server for the SMTP. For that you need to export the certificate from the Exchange 2013 where you had complete the certificate request. Check the step of exporting and importing in google and one can follow the steps given on MS site and/or more easier on some leading blogs which for copyright reasons I cannot explicitly mention in this book.
I am using wildcard cert of digicert.

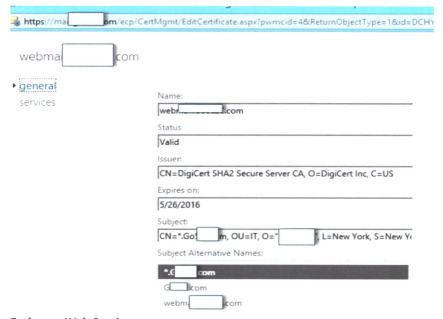

Exchange Web Services:
We assume that you have already configured External url on Exchange 2013 CAS servers for Exchange Web Services (EWS), Outlook Address Book (OAB), Outlook Web App (OWA), Exchange Control Panel (ECP), and the Exchange ActiveSync (Microsoft-Server-ActiveSync) virtual directories in the internet facing AD site.
At the same time we need to ensure that you enable the MRS proxy service on the internet facing Client Access servers as part of EWS configuration. To enable the MRS proxy service, do the following:

- Open the EAC and navigate to **Servers** > **Virtual directories**.
- Select the Client Access server, select the **EWS** virtual directory, and

then click **Edit**

- Select the **MRS Proxy enabled** check box, and then click **Save**.
- Make sure to do it on all internet facing CAS servers one by one.

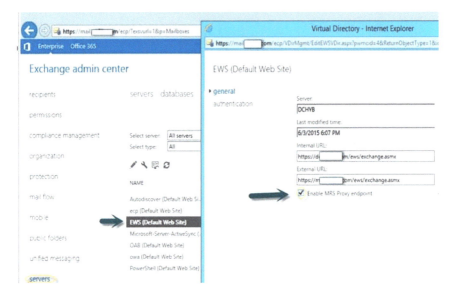

Hybrid Configuration Wizard The Hybrid Configuration wizard helps you establish your hybrid deployment by creating the *HybridConfiguration* object in your on-premises Active Directory and gathering existing Exchange & Active Directory topology configuration data. The Hybrid Configuration Wizard also enables you to define & configure several organization parameters for your hybrid deployment, including secure mail transport options.

➢ Login to the Exchange 2013 Server and login to ECP.
➢ Click on **Hybrid** then click on **enable** to start the wizard.

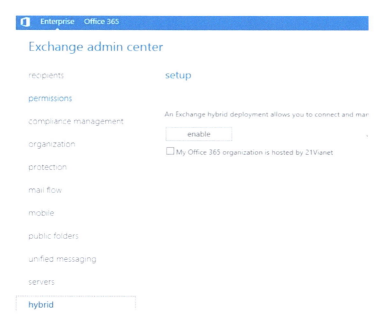

"My Office 365 organization is hosted by 21Vianet" – If you are based in China then you need to check this checkbox, else ignore this checkbox. If your Office 365 tenant is hosted by 21Vianet & this checkbox isn't selected, the Hybrid Configuration wizard won't connect to 21Vianet service, your Office 365 account credentials won't be recognized & the wizard won't complete properly.

➢ Click on sign in to office 365

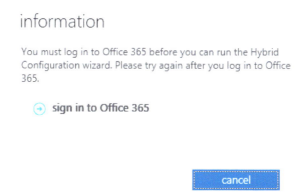

➢ Login to office 365 portal. You need to enable the cookies to sign in to office 365, else you will see this error.

412
Cookies Are Disabled :(

To use this service, you have to enable cookies in your Web browser settings. For information about how to enable cookies, see Help for your Web browser.

This is how you enable the cookies.

Refresh here and it will replace the URL with the following. Domain is your domain.

https://outlook.office365.com/ecp/hybrid.aspx?xprs=*mail.domain.com*&xprf=01&xprv=15.0.1076.11&realm=microsoftonline.com&exsvurl=1&ov=1&mkt=en-US&op=Setup&wa=wsignin1.0

> ➢ Now you should be able to switch between the "**Enterprise**" and "**Office 365**" modes without the need to authenticate.

Look at this I can see my office 365 admin accounts

> ➢ Click again on enable and click yes when prompted. Now it is back to your URL.

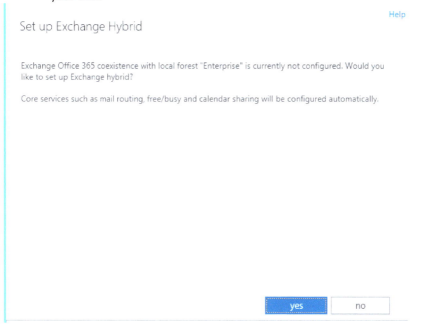

> ➢ Copy the token and create DNS txt record.

Set up Exchange Hybrid

Exchange Office 365 coexistence with local forest "Enterprise" hybrid configuration in progress.

Before proceeding to the next step, copy the following tokens and create a TXT record for each token on your public DNS to confirm domain ownership.

DOMAIN	TOKEN

I have created the DNS TXT record and clicked next on my hybrid wizard

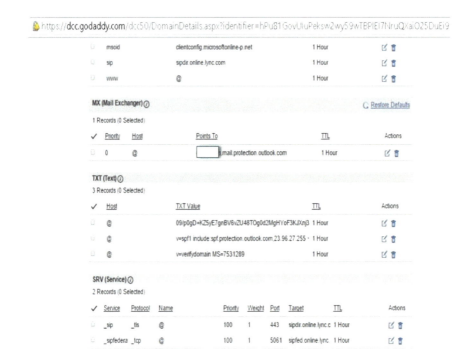

> ➢ This step is asking us how we want to route the email. If you have Edge Transport then select to route emails through edge transport else keep client Access and mailbox server.

When you click on more options you will another option if you enable this then you will receive all outgoing internet emails on your on premise exchange to send them to internet. To enable this feature select the **Enable centralized mail transport** check box in the **More options** section. The on-premises transport servers will be responsible for delivering the messages to external recipients. This approach is helpful in compliance scenarios where all mail to and from the Internet must be processed by on-premises servers. If this check box is not selected, the Exchange Online organization will deliver messages to external recipients directly.

I am going ahead with default setting as I don't have Edge in this setup and I don't have compliance setup or requirement.

Help

Modify Exchange Hybrid

How do you want to configure your on-premises organization for secure bi-directional mail transport with your Exchange Online organization? Learn more

◉ Configure my Client Access and Mailbox servers for secure mail transport (typical)

◯ Configure my Edge Transport servers for secure mail transport

Centralized mail transport is an advanced feature that most organizations will not require. Enabling this feature configures your Exchange Online organization to route email to or from external recipients through your on-premises Exchange organization. Please see the Exchange setup guide for more details. Learn more

☐ Enable centralized mail transport

➢ Now add your Exchange 2013 Hybrid CAS Servers on which receive connectors will be created and click next.

Modify Exchange Hybrid

Choose one or more on-premises Client Access servers to host Receive connectors for secure bi-directional mail transport with Exchange Online. Learn more

Receiving Client Access servers:

DCHYB   ✕   browse...

➢ Now add the Exchange 2013 Mailbox servers which will host the send connector and click next.

Modify Exchange Hybrid

Choose one or more on-premises Mailbox servers to host Send connectors for secure bi-directional mail transport with Exchange Online. Learn more

Sending Mailbox servers:

DCHYB   ✕   browse...

> ➢ Select the certificate from dropdown list for the secure mail transport. The certificate should be issued by a trusted CA provider

This list displays the digital certificates issued by a third-party certificate authority (CA) installed on the Mailbox server(s) selected in the previous step. Click next.

> ➢ Now type the externally accessible FQDN for the on-premises Client Access server(s). The EOP service in Office 365 uses this FQDN to configure the service connectors for secure mail transport between your Exchange organizations.

You may need to specify which domain is the primary domain which will be used for Autodiscover in case your exchange org has multiple primary SMTP domains. By doing so we can eliminate the need for both adding "autodiscover.domain.com" for all SMTP domains to a SAN certificate as well as the need for publishing Autodiscover for each of these.

Run the below command to configure an SMTP domain as the Autodiscover domain, basically you need to add autod: in front of the domain:

Set-HybridConfiguration –Domains "autod:domainUSA.com, domainAsia.com, domainAU.com"

> ➢ Provide on Premise credentials which are member of Organization Management group.

Modify Exchange Hybrid

Exchange hybrid setup needs both on-premises and Office 365 account credentials before it can continue. Both accounts must be members of the Organization Management role group. Learn more

Enter your on-premises account credentials.

*Domain\user name:

    \ADFS2SVC

*Password:

    •••••••••

> Provide office 365 credentials which are member of Organization Management and global administrator group.

Modify Exchange Hybrid

Exchange hybrid setup needs both on-premises and Office 365 account credentials before it can continue. Both accounts must be members of the Organization Management role group. Learn more

Enter your Office 365 credentials.

*Office 365 user ID:

    abc@123.com _

*Password:

    ••••••••••

> We have completed the configuration settings. Now click on update to configure and enable the hybrid features.

Modify Exchange Hybrid

Your Exchange hybrid configuration settings are now complete. Click Update to configure and enable the hybrid features in your Enterprise and Office 365 organizations.

This process may take several minutes to complete. Please don't close the window unless you want to cancel the process.

Configure Organization Relationship

Click 'Stop' to cancel the operation. Stopping the operation won't undo the changes already applied.

- ➤ **Hybrid Setup completed** After the initial hybrid deployment configuration steps are complete, the wizard displays a message to complete the connection with Office 365 and configure Exchange OAuth authentication. Select **Configure** to connect to Office 365 and start the OAuth configuration wizard.
- ➤ **OAuth** is an open standard for authorization **OAuth** provides client applications a 'secure delegated Access' to server resources on behalf of a resource owner. It specifies a process for resource owners to authorize third-party access to their server resources without sharing their credentials.
- ➤ **You may like to stop here** but I am running it to show what comes next.

Modify Exchange Hybrid

Your Exchange hybrid deployment configuration is almost complete!

Exchange hybrid setup needs to connect to your Office 365 tenant to complete the OAuth authentication configuration process. Selecting configure below will take you to your Office 365 tenant and start the configuration process. Learn more

- ➤ Click on configure on this screen to start the OAuth authentication.

Exchange Hybrid Configuration

To configure your on-premises Exchange and Office 365 organizations for OAuth authentication, select configure to start the download for the application. If prompted, select run to install the application.

Click here to learn what this feature does

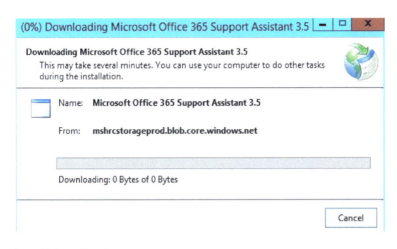

➢ Click on Run here.

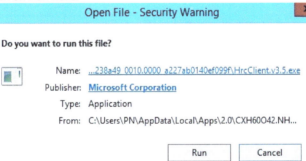

➢ Click on Run again.

Click on Run again.

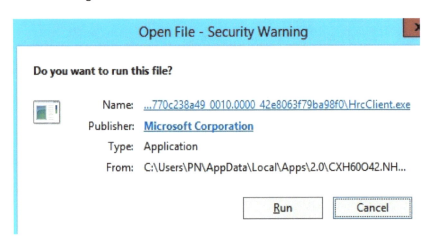

> ➢ And Done. If you have reached here then you will be very happy right now.

Exchange Hybrid Configuration

Your hybrid configuration is complete. You can close this browser window now.

Done

Access the Exchange online Organization in Exchange 2013 EAC

You access the Exchange Online organization in the EAC by selecting the Office

365 cross-premises navigation tab. From there you can easily switch between your Exchange Online and your on-premises Exchange organizations.

- ➢ Open the EAC on an Exchange 2013 server.
- ➢ In the EAC, select the **Office 365** cross-premises navigation tab.
- ➢ Verify that the EAC displays objects for the Exchange Online organization.

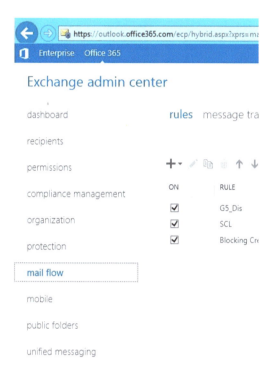

Follow the steps in MS KB jj984289 for steps to connect to exchange using PowerShell if you are comfortable and happy using it.

IMPORTANT STEP – Don't SKIP ! - Review the hybrid configuration

Review the current configuration:

Hybrid configuration: Run the following command to get Hybrid configuration - Get-HybridConfiguration

We can see the settings (such as receiving and sending transport servers, on-premises smart host and domains) we specified when we ran the Hybrid wizard have been set on the hybrid configuration object. We can also see which features have been enabled ("**FreeBusy**", "**MoveMailbox**", "**MailTips**", "**MessageTracking**", "**OwaRedirection**", "**OnlineArchive**", "**SecureMail**", "**Photos**"), which are all features we wish to have enabled between the on-premises Exchange organization and the Exchange Online organization in Office 365.

The "**ClientAccessServers**" parameter is deprecated and will be removed in future updates of Exchange Server 2013, which is why it is blank.

"**EdgeTransportServers**" attributes is blank because we are not using it.

"**CentralizedTransport**" is missing under "**Features**" because we did not select it.

Federation Trust

A federation trust with the Microsoft Federation Gateway has been established for the specified domain:

Creating a federation trust with the MFG is required in order to be able to set up an organizational relationship, which again is required in order to share free/busy information and calendars between the on-premises Exchange organization Office 365. There is no trust setup with the MFG, instead the MFG just acts as a trust broker.

Similarly on the office 365 side we have following Federation

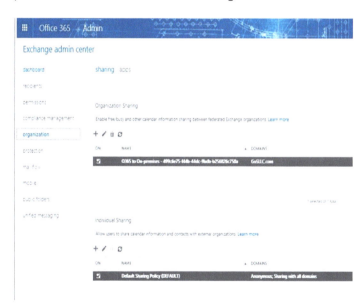

Organization Relationship: We can see there is an org relationship has been build. By default, free/busy, mailbox moves, delivery reports, mail tips and online archive are enabled.

There is targetOWAURL attribute specified and by default, which is set to: "http://outlook.com/owa/tenant_name.onmicrosoft.com". The target OWA

URL is the URL that a user will be non-transparently redirected, when he tries to access his mailbox using the existing OWA namespace (i.e. http://mail.domain.com/owa) after his mailbox has been moved to Office 365.

Exchange On-Premise to Office 365: Flawless ActiveSync Migration
Microsoft has found a new way to migrate and update active sync URL when we migrate from on premise to office 365.

All on premise migration has always been flawless but when we used to migrate to office 365, we had required to update the active sync device manually if DNS pointing to on premise.
With the newly released Exchange 2013 CU13 (8 and above) and Exchange 2010 SP3 RU9, it is possible to update the active sync device with the new URL of office 365.
This is how it works now.
1. Migrate the mailbox from on premise to office 365.
2. ActiveSync device tries to sync using the currently configured URL which connects to on-premises Client Access server. This can be Exchange 2010 or 2013 CAS.
3. This Client Access server further queries Domain controller to check if the user mailbox is present.
4. Then Client Access server gets a response from Domain controller that the user mailbox is not found.
5. Then Client Access server queries to find the "TargetOWAURL" attribute present on the organization relationship object for the Office 365configuration.
The "RemoteRoutingAddress" attribute present on the remote mailbox which is used to find the correct organization relationship.
6. So here Client Access server receives the TargetOWAURL configured on the Organization Relationship.
7. Now Client Access server sends the URL in an HTTP 451 response to the mobile device. Device should support HTTP 451 redirection.
8. The active sync device tries to sync with the new URL.
9. The active sync profile on the device is updated to the Office 365 URL.
Let us know more about these 2 attributes.
1. **TargetOWAURL:**
The TargetOwaURL parameter specifies the Microsoft Office Outlook Web App URL of the external organization defined in the organization relationship. It is used for Outlook Web App redirection in a cross-premise Exchange scenario. Configuring this attribute enables users in the organization to use their current Outlook Web App URL to access Outlook Web App in the external organization.
Now ActiveSync migration process also use the same url to connect to your office 365.

2. **RemoteRoutingAddress:**

The *RemoteRoutingAddress* parameter specifies the SMTP address of the mailbox in the service that this user is associated with.

If you've configured mail flow between the on-premises organization and the service, you don't need to specify this parameter. The remote routing address is calculated automatically. "RemoreRoutingAddress" is a "TargetAddress" Attribute configured on an on premise mail enabled user.

At the same time this URL should be resolving office 365 URL.

The targetautodiscoverEpr has been set by the HCW. This is the endpoint used to reach out to the Exchange Online organization for the configured features, when a request comes from the on-premises Exchange organization to office 365.

And in office 365 it looks like below:

```
PS C:\Users\PN> Get-OrganizationRelationship | fl

RunspaceId              : a981dc76-1711-4c3e-9b28-dc9f972558ca
DomainNames             : {          com}
FreeBusyAccessEnabled   : True
FreeBusyAccessLevel     : LimitedDetails
FreeBusyAccessScope     :
MailboxMoveEnabled      : False
DeliveryReportEnabled   : True
MailTipsAccessEnabled   : True
MailTipsAccessLevel     : All
MailTipsAccessScope     :
PhotosEnabled           : True
TargetApplicationUri    : FYDIBOHF25SPDLT.
TargetSharingEpr        :
TargetOwaURL            :
TargetAutodiscoverEpr   : https://autodiscover.         com/autodiscover/autodiscover.svc/WSSecurity
OrganizationContact     :
Enabled                 : True
ArchiveAccessEnabled    : False
AdminDisplayName        :
ExchangeVersion         : 0.10 (14.0.100.0)
Name                    : O365 to On-premises - 499c6e75-f44b-44dc-9bdb-b256826c750a
DistinguishedName       : CN=O365 to On-premises - 499c6e75-f44b-44dc-9bdb-b256826c750a,CN=Federation,CN=Configuration,CN
                          .CN=ConfigurationUnits,DC=NAMPR08A001,DC=prod,DC=outlook,DC=com
Identity                : O365 to On-premises - 499c6e75-f44b-44dc-9bdb-b256826c750a
Guid                    : 84518684-7977-418b-ac7d-a3a0e0d75874
ObjectCategory          : NAMPR08A001.prod.outlook.com/Configuration/Schema/ms-Exch-Fed-Sharing-Relationship
ObjectClass             : {top,          haringRelationship}
WhenChanged             : 6/19/2015 5:18:55 AM
WhenCreated             : 6/19/2015 5:18:49 AM
WhenChangedUTC          : 6/19/2015 9:18:55 AM
WhenCreatedUTC          : 6/19/2015 9:18:49 AM
OrganizationId          : NAMPR08A001.prod.outlook.com/Microsoft Exchange Hosted
                          Organizations,          onmicrosoft.com -
                          NAMPR08A001.prod.outlook.com/ConfigurationUnits/ExchangeWizkid.onmicrosoft.com/Configuration
Id                      : O365 to On-premises - 499c6e75-f44b-44dc-9bdb-b256826c750a
OriginatingServer       : BY2PR08A001DC01.NAMPR08A001.prod.outlook.com
IsValid                 : True
ObjectState             : Unchanged
```

By default, free/busy, delivery reports, photos and mailtips are enabled. TargetautodiscoverEpr has been set by the HCW. This is the endpoint used to reach out to the on-premises Exchange organization for the configured features.

Accepted domain: Hybrid wizard has added
this **"tenant_name.mail.onmicrosoft.com"** in the accepted domain of
Exchange 2013 and office 365. Office 365 should be authoritative and on
Exchange 2013 should be internal relay.

Email Address Policy: We can see "**tenant_name.mail.onmicrosoft.com**" has been added to default email address policy which means it will be added to all the users proxy addresses for mail routing.

➢

We can also see x500 address has stamped on the synced users which is office365 address.

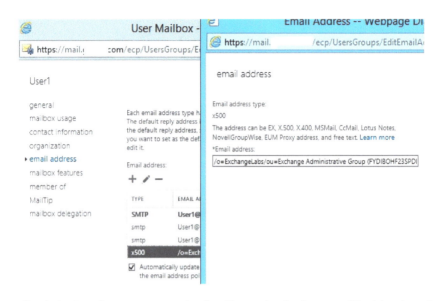

Check the Receive connectors: Looks like only 2 changes "Enable domain security (mutual auth TLS)" and "Anonymous users" on the Default Receive connector on the Frontend connector.

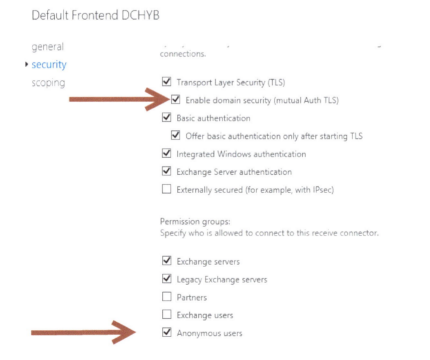

Check the Send Connectors

I got new send connector which has my office 365 master domain and it is going to use MX record.

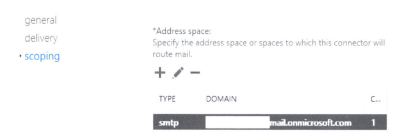

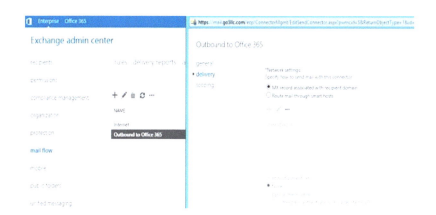

This means all office 365 users will have Target address set to this master domain address.

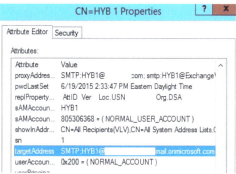

Connectors at Office 365 - I got 2 connectors in the office 365.

Let us see what we have in it.

Inbound connector: This is the inbound connector with certificate which will be used to verify on premise Exchange 2013 email server.

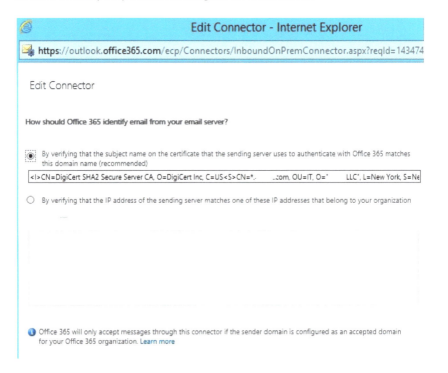

Outbound Connector:

Remember Hybrid wizard asked for the FQDN of the SMTP server. It is configured here.

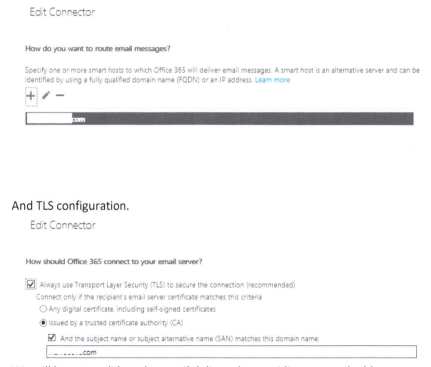

And TLS configuration.

We will have to validate the email delivery by providing an email address. Select the connector and click on validation on the right side.

Specify the email id and click validate.

You should see this screen in few minutes with both succeeded.

Now the validation status will be Successful

Remote Domain: "Tenant_name.mail.onmicrosoft.com" has been added in the remote domain as well.

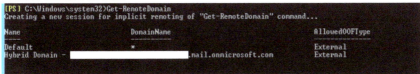

This has following configuration

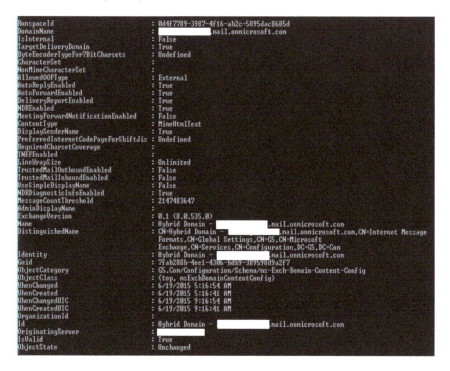

Ports and URLS: Make sure the following ports are URLS are open from internet.

URLs	DNS Record type	Public IP/hostname	Ports	Protocol	Server
mail.domain.com	host	x.x.x.1	443 & 25	TCP	Exchange 2013 CAS+MBX
autodiscover.domain.com	host/alias	x.x.x.1	443	TCP	Exchange 2013 CAS+MBX
@	mx	mail.domain.com	25	TCP	Exchange 2013 CAS+M

					BX
fs.domain.com	host	x.x.x.2	443	TCP	ADFS and AADSync Server
enterpriseregistration.domain.com	host/alias	x.x.x.2	443	TCP	ADFS and AADSync Server

My DNS records look like this.

CNAME (Alias) ☑

	Host	Points to
✔		
☐	azaad	fs .com
☐	email	email.secureserver.net
☐	enterprisere...	fs. com
☐	ftp	@
☐	lyncdiscover	webdir.online.lync.com
☐	msoid	clientconfig.microsoftonline-p.net
☐	sip	sipdir.online.lync.com
☐	www	@

A (Host) ☑

	Host	Points to
✔		
☐	@	50.63.202.44
☐	autodiscover	23.96.125.188
☐	fs	23.96.102.145
☐	mail	23.96.125.188

MX (Mail Exchanger) ☑

	Priority	Host	Points to
✔			
☐	0	@	-com.mail.protection.outlook.com
☐	0	@	mail. com

⊙ Quick Add

TXT (Text) ☑

	Host	TXT Value
✔		
☐	@	09/p0gD+KZ5yE7gnBV6vZU48TOg0d2MgHYoF3KJXnj...
☐	@	v=spf1 include:spf.protection.outlook.com,...
☐	@	v=verifydomain MS=7531289

⊙ Quick Add   Add SPF Record

SRV (Service) ☑

	Service	Protocol	Name	Priority
✔				
☐	_sip	_tls	@	100
☐	_sipfederationtls	_tcp	@	100

Mailboxes - Migration To Online + Creating New Ones Online

Create Office 365 account from On-Premise Exchange 2013 EAC

You can use the Office 365 Mailbox wizard in the EAC on an Exchange server to create a mailbox in the Exchange Online organization. If you want to create more than one test mailbox, you'll have to use this wizard for each mailbox. You can't use the wizard to create multiple mailboxes at one time.

- Open Exchange 2013 EAC and click **Recipients** in the feature pane for the Enterprise organization.
- In the feature tabs, click **Mailboxes**.
- Expand the menu at the **Add** control and select **Office 365 mailbox.** This has been added by the Hybrid wizard we ran earlier.

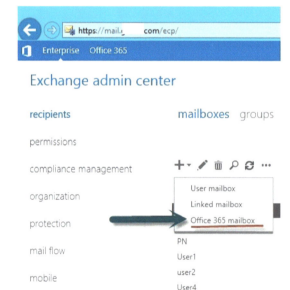

- On the **New Office 365 mailbox** page, specify the following settings:
  - ➢ **First Name**
  - ➢ **Last Name**
  - ➢ **User logon name** Type the user logon name of the new user and select the primary SMTP domain used for your other on-premises users
  - ➢ **Mailbox type** Choose the type of mailbox to create.
  - ➢ **Password** Type the password.
  - ➢ **Confirm password** Retype the password.
  - ➢ Make sure the **Create an archive mailbox** check box is not selected.

- Click **Save** to continue. You will see the mailbox type is Office 365.

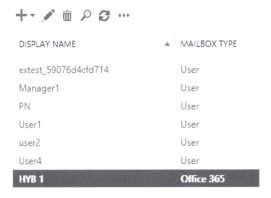

- Force the DirSync. To force immediate directory synchronization, open a command prompt with elevated privileges and start the DirectorySyncClientCmd tool from C:Program Files\Microsoft Azure AD SyncBin:

Important: If you have configure group based ADsync filtering then don't forget to Add this user as a member of the group, else your AADsync will not pick it.

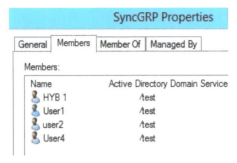

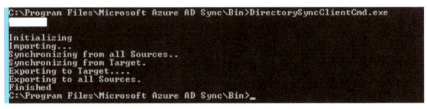

- Log on to: Cloud-based service administration portal

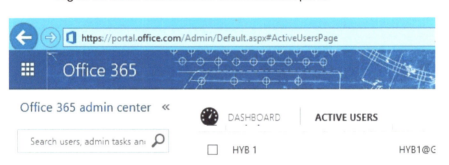

- Assign a license to the new user.

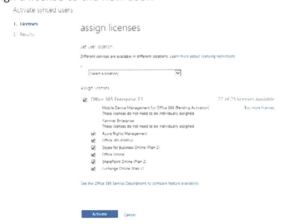

Move a Mailbox from Exchange 2013 to Office 365

- **Wizard move for single batch with multiple mailboxes:**

We will use the remote move migration wizard in the Office 365 tab in the Exchange admin center (EAC) on an Exchange 2013 server to move existing user mailboxes in the on-premises organization to the Exchange Online organization (office 365):

Open the EAC and navigate to **Office 365 migration**.

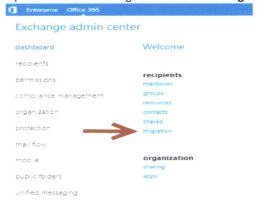

Click **Add** and select **Migrate to Exchange Online**.

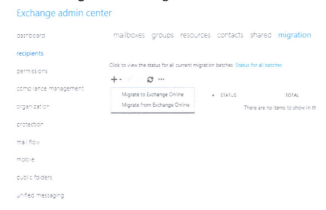

On the **Select a migration type** page, select **Remote move** and then click **Next**.

On the **Select the users** page, click **Add**, select the on-premises users to move to Office 365 or provide a csv file and click **Add**, and then click **OK**. Click **Next**.

On the **Enter the Windows user account credential** page, enter the on-premises administrator authentication. Click Next.

new migration batch
Enter on-premises account credentials

Account with privileges (domain\user name):

\ADFS2SVC

Password of account with privileges:

••••••••|

On the **Confirm the migration endpoint** page, verify that the FDQN of your on-premises Client Access server is listed when the wizard confirms the migration endpoint. Click **Next**.

The total time to complete the mailbox move depends on the total number of mailboxes selected, the size of the mailboxes, and the properties of the

MRSProxy.

On the **Move configuration** page, enter a name for the migration batch.
Use the down arrow to select the target delivery domain for the mailboxes that are migrating to Office 365. In most hybrid deployments, this will be the primary SMTP domain used for both on-premises and Exchange Online organization mailboxes. Verify that the **Move primary mailbox along with archive mailbox** option is selected because we just don't want to move the archive mailbox, and then click **Next**. We can also assign baditemlimit and largeitemlimit.

On the **Start the batch** page, select at least one recipient to receive the batch complete report where you can assign an external recipient as well. Verify that the **automatically start the batch** option is selected, and then select the **automatically complete the migration batch** radio button selected. Click **New**.

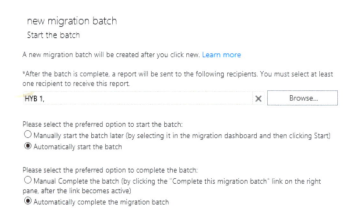

Look at this options, we can migrate the data offline and when complete the move later. This will migrate 95% of the data.

"Manual Complete the batch (by clicking the "Complete this migration batch" link on the right pane, after the link becomes active) @NewMigrationBatch_ManuallyComplete"

While the mailboxes are being moved, you will see a status of **Syncing** in the migration status for each mailbox moved to Office 365. After the mailbox move request reaches a status of **Completed**, the mailbox migration process is complete.

Now we can see moves have completed.

And we got the email to inform us, migration has completed. So you don't need to check the status of the migration again and again.

Migration batch 1st Move has completed successfully.

Microsoft Outlook
Fri 6/19/2015 9:31 PM

To: Architects GoldenFive; HYB 1;

Migration batch 1st Move has completed successfully.

Synced:	Mailboxes - 2
	All mailboxes completely migrated
Total mailboxes:	Mailboxes - 2

Click here to download the success report. You may be required to sign in.

Click on the delete to clear the move batch request.

Office 365 creates endpoint which does not remove even after clearing the migration request. Exchange 2013 uses the same endpoint for multiple migrations. Click on ... on the migration under office 365 or run the command Get-Migrationendpoint | fl on office 365 connected PowerShell.

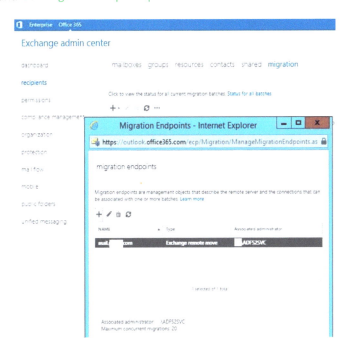

After the migration On Exchange 2013 mailboxes will look like this.

Office 365 will show like this

Mailbox move using PowerShell command:

Connect to the Office 365
Define variables
Provide office 365 credential

$O365Cred = Get-credential
Provide on Premise Exchange 2013 credential
$2013Cred = Get-credential

Run the command to connect to the Azure AD.
Connect-MsolService -Credential $O365CRED

Exchange 2013 creates Migration Endpoint which it does not remove and allow to you the same Endpoint.

Prepare a csv file with email addresses which will look like the below screen

Get the already created migration end point with the following command

$MigEndpoint = Get-MigrationEndpoint

```
PS C:\Users\PN.G5\Desktop> $MigEndpoint = Get-MigrationEndpoint
PS C:\Users\PN.G5\Desktop> $MigEndpoint = Get-MigrationEndpoint
```

Run the below command to create a batch for migration. I have mark the values which you will change according to your configuration.

New-MigrationBatch -Name "Name of theMigrationBatch" -SourceEndpoint $MigEndpoint.Identity -TargetDeliveryDomain yourdomain.mail.onmicrosoft.com -CSVData ([System.IO.File]::ReadAllBytes("C:tempinput.csv"))

* Example command *

New-MigrationBatch -Name Mig2 -SourceEndpoint $MigEndpoint.Identity -TargetDeliveryDomain yourdomain.mail.onmicrosoft.com -CSVData ([System.IO.File]::ReadAllBytes("C:tempinput.csv"))

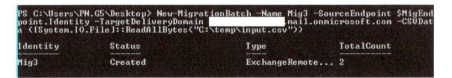

There are 2 more parameter which can eliminate the need of further command

Autostart - The AutoStart parameter specifies whether to immediately start the processing of the new migration batch. If you don't use the AutoStart parameter, you have to manually start the migration batch by using the **Start-MigrationBatch** cmdlet.

AutoComplete - The AutoComplete parameter specifies whether to force the finalization of the individual mailboxes in a migration batch when the initial synchronization for a mailbox is successfully completed. Alternatively, you have

to run the **Complete-MigrationBatch** cmdlet to finalize a migration batch. This parameter can only be used for local moves and remote move migrations.
This parameter will force the individual mailboxes to be finalized as soon as the mailbox has completed initial synchronization.
This command is without the parameter -AutoComplete will suspend the move at 95%. This parameter allows you to move the data on the backend without interrupting users until they are ready for migration.

Run the below command to start the migration sync. This will not complete the migration
Start-MigrationBatch -Identity Mig2

Got the email initial sync has completed

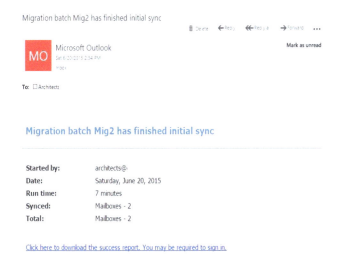

Run the below command to monitor the move.

Get-MigrationBatch

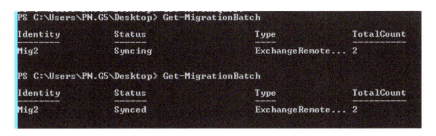

Once you see the migration has synced, run the below command.

Complete-MigrationBatch -Identity Mig2

Now you will batch is completing the migration.

Got the email migration has completed

Migration batch Mig2 has completed successfully.

← Reply   ← Reply all   → Forward   ...

MO Microsoft Outlook
Sat 6/20/2015 2:54 PM

Mark as unread

To: ☐ Architects

Migration batch Mig2 has completed successfully.

Synced:	Mailboxes - 2 All mailboxes completely migrated
Total mailboxes:	Mailboxes - 2

Click here to download the success report. You may be required to sign in.

When I click the migration report. We got this link

Download Migration Report

The migration report, in CSV format, will begin downloading momentarily. If the download doesn't start in the next 30 seconds, click Start download

Which downloads a csv file with the below info.

EmailAddress	Status	ItemsMigrated	ItemsSkipped
user5@ com	complete	2	0
user6@_ com	complete	2	0

We can also check the migration configuration by running the below command

Get-MigrationConfig | FL

```
PS C:\Users\PN.___\Desktop> Get-MigrationConfig ! FL

RunspaceId           : 156fa971-e1d8-459c-a673-a8e4d6a57d82
Identity             : _____.onmicrosoft.com
MaxNumberOfBatches   : 100
MaxConcurrentMigrations : 100
Features             : MultiBatch
CanSubmitNewBatch    : True
SupportsCutover      : False
IsValid              : True
ObjectState          : Unchanged
```

We can use **Set-MigrationConfig** to change any parameter.

Parameter	Required	Type	Description
Confirm	Optional	System.Management.Automation.SwitchParameter	The Confirm switch causes the command to pause processing and requires you to acknowledge what the command will do before processing continues. You don't have to specify a value with the Confirm switch.
DomainController	Optional	Microsoft.Exchange.Data.Fqdn	The DomainController parameter specifies the fully qualified domain name (FQDN) of the domain controller that writes this configuration change to Active Directory.
Features	Optional	Microsoft.Exchange.Data.Storage.Management.MigrationFeature	The Features parameter specifies the set of features to enable for the migration system. Use one of the following values: • None • MultiBatch • Endorsums • UpgradedLicov
Identity	Optional	Microsoft.Exchange.Management.Migration.MigrationConfig.cParameter	This parameter is reserved for internal Microsoft use.
MaxConcurrentMigrations	Optional	Microsoft.Exchange.Data.Unlimited	The MaxConcurrentMigrations parameter specifies the maximum number of active migrations that your organization can run at any specific time
MaxNumberOfBatches	Optional	System.Int32	The MaxNumberOfBatches parameter specifies the maximum number of batches that your organization can migrate at any time
Partner	Optional	Microsoft.Exchange.Configuration.Tasks.MailboxIdParameter	This parameter is reserved for internal Microsoft use.
WhatIf	Optional	System.Management.Automation.SwitchParameter	The WhatIf switch instructs the command to simulate the actions that it would take on the object. By using the WhatIf switch, you can view what changes would occur without having to apply any of those changes. You don't have to specify a value with the WhatIf switch.

This command will show the statistics of the mailbox migration

Get-MigrationUser | Get-MigrationUserStatistics | FL

As expected mailbox moved and type changed Office 365.

Move a Mailbox without Batch from PowerShell

Run the following commands in the same PowerShell
New-MoveRequest -Identity "Alias" -Remote -RemoteHostName
"MRSProxyURL" -TargetDeliveryDomain domainname.mail.onmicrosoft.com -
RemoteCredential $SourceCRED -BadItemLimit 0

Example

New-MoveRequest -Identity "Chetan" -Remote -RemoteHostName
"mail.cp.com" -TargetDeliveryDomain Cp.mail.onmicrosoft.com -
RemoteCredential $2013Cred -BadItemLimit 0

Move a Mailbox from Office 365 to Exchange 2013

We can use the remote move migration wizard on the **Office 365** tab in the
Exchange 2013 EAC on any Exchange server to move existing user mailboxes in
the Exchange Online organization to the on-premises organization:

1. Open the EAC and navigate to **Office 365 Recipients migration**.
2. Click **Add ✚** then select **Migrate from Exchange Online**.

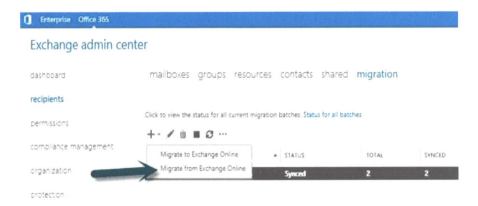

3. Select the users that you want to move and click Next

4. On the **Select the users** page, click **Add** ➕ and then select the Exchange Online users to move to the on-premises organization, click **Add** and then click **OK**. Click **Next**.

5. On the **Confirm the migration endpoint** page, verify that the FDQN of your on-premises Client Access server is listed then click next.

new migration batch
Confirm the migration endpoint

The connection settings for this migration batch have been automatically selected based on the migration endpoints created in your organization. Learn more

Remote MRS proxy server:
The FQDN of the Exchange server that the Mailbox Replication Service (MRS) Proxy is on.

| mail._____com |

6. On the **Move configuration** page, enter the following

Required
New migration batch name
Target delivery domain
Target database
Bad item limit

Optional
Target archive database
Large item limit

new migration batch
Move configuration

These configuration settings will be applied to the new batch. Learn more

*New migration batch name:

Batch3

*Target delivery domain:

    com   ˅

Archive:
◉ Move the primary mailbox and the archive mailbox if one exists

○ Move primary mailbox only, without moving archive mailbox
   This option is only valid for mailboxes on Exchange 2010 and Exchange 2013.

*Target database:
Enter the database name you'd like to move this mailbox to:

Mailbox Database 0752943666

Target archive database:
Enter the database name you'd like to move the archive mailbox to:

Bad item limit:

Large item limit:

Don't give DB name with inverted commas ("") else you will receive the below error

Error: MigrationPermanentException: The Mailbox Replication Service was unable to find the remote database. –> The Mailbox Replication Service was unable to find the remote database. –> The call to 'https://mail.cp.com/EWS/mrsproxy.svc' failed because no service was listening on the specified endpoint. Error details: There was no endpoint listening at https://mail.cp.com/EWS/mrsproxy.svc that could accept the message. This is often caused by an incorrect address or SOAP action. See InnerException, if present, for more details. –> The remote server returned an error: (404) Not Found. –> There was no endpoint listening at https://mail.cp.com/EWS/mrsproxy.svc that could accept the message. This is often caused by an incorrect address or SOAP action. See InnerException, if present, for more details. –> The remote server returned an error: (404) Not Found.

7. On the **Start the batch** page, add one recipient to receive the batch complete report.

Verify that **automatically start the batch** is selected and select the **automatically complete the migration batch** then Click **New**.

new migration batch

Start the batch

A new migration batch will be created after you click new. Learn more

*After the batch is complete, a report will be sent to the following recipients. You must select at least
one recipient to receive this report.

| HYB 1 | ✕ | Browse... |

Please select the preferred option to start the batch:
○ Manually start the batch later (by selecting it in the migration dashboard and then clicking Start)
◉ Automatically start the batch

Please select the preferred option to complete the batch:
○ Manual Complete the batch (by clicking the "Complete this migration batch" link on the right
pane, after the link becomes active)
◉ Automatically complete the migration batch

8. **Now you will see the migrations has completed and mailbox type has
converted from Office 365 to user.**

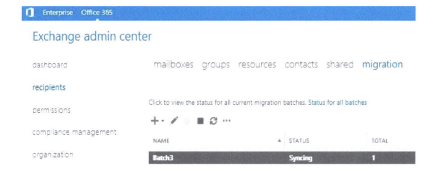

And the move completed.

Post move login

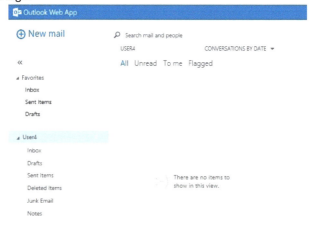

Mail flow   I have tested the mailflow from office 365 to Exchange 2013, Exchange 2013 to office 365, office 365 to Internet, Exchange 2013 to Internet and Internet to Exchange 2013.

From Office 365 to Exchange 2013 on-premise
Internet to Office 365 to Exchange 2013 on-Premise
From Exchange 2013 on-premise to Office 365
From Office 365 to Internet
From Exchange 2013 on-premise to Internet

All mailflow working as expected.

Post Migration Tasks:
There are certain change required post configuration and migration. Let us walkthrough what are the changes required.

Change MX record

After you've completed configuration of your hybrid deployment using the Hybrid Configuration wizard and validated the outbound connector in office 365 then you can direct mail flow through the Exchange Online Protection (EOP). At the same time we have 3 options which are mentioned below:
1. Let the incoming mailflow continue as it is. In this case no changes required and Exchange 2013 will forward the emails to the office 365 mailboxes using the targetaddress attribute which migration will set.
2. Add 2nd mx record which will point to Exchange online Protection. In this case we will add high availability to our design. Targetaddress attribute will forward the email from On-premise to office 365 and office 365 will also forward to Exchange 2013.
3. Final option is change the mx record pointer to the Exchange online Protection. This will be the only option left when we will be decommissioning Exchange servers. After you change the MX record to point to the EOP mail servers, all email messages for both on-premises and Exchange Online recipients will be routed through EOP and Exchange Online. Email messages for on-premises recipients will then be routed from Exchange Online to your on-premises organization.

MX record for Exchange Online Protection will be setup like this

TYPE	PRIORITY	HOST NAME	POINTS TO ADDRESS	TTL
MX	0	@	-com.mail.protection.outlook.com	1 Hour

If you want to see what different options are available for Hybrid Transport then please search for MS KB jj659055 - TechNet link on Hybrid Transport.

Reverse Migration Issue

If you have created a mailbox in Office 365 and trying to migrate it to Exchange 2013 on-premise then you need to update ExchangeGuid in the remote mailbox Properties by running the following command before starting the move of this mailbox.

Set-REmoteMailbox mailboxname –ExchangeGuid Guid

```
[PS] C:\Windows\system32>set-RemoteMailbox hyb1 -ExchangeGuid 22d36920-2d00-4a0e-b5e1-63247fdf7b07
[PS] C:\Windows\system32>
```

To get the GUID you need to connect to the office 365 from windows PowerShell and run the command.

Get-mailbox mailboxname | fl ExchangeGuid
Refer – MS KB 2956029

Testing your Hybrid:

EXRCA.com (exchange remote connectivity analyzer) is the best place to run office 365 test. I ran SingleSignOn test and I got passed.

You can use to analyze, and run tests for, several Exchange 2013 and Office 365 services, including Exchange Web Services, Outlook, Exchange ActiveSync, and Internet email connectivity.

OWA and ActiveSync Mailbox Policies

We can configure OWA and ActiveSync mailbox policies as per our requirement. By default, default policy will be assigned.

Remote Domain

You can add additional remote domain and configure their policy as per on-premise configuration..

Client Connectivity:

Let us also have a look on the client connectivity so that we can see how client experience.

Users running Outlook 2013, Outlook 2010, or Outlook 2007 who connect using

Outlook Anywhere will be automatically reconfigured to connect to the Exchange Online organization when their mailbox is moved.

ActiveSync users will be automatically configured if their Exchange and device level support this feature.

ActiveSync Configuration Options

Migration from Exchange 2013 to Office 365

You don't need to configure mobile device because Targetowaurl attribute will provide redirection URL. I have tested this and it works but have some patience because it may take 5-10 minutes.

Migration from Office 365 to Exchange 2013

If you have to migrate back from office 365 to Exchange 2013 then you may like to try the following but Microsoft has confirmed that it will not work and I have not got any success either.

Get-OrganizationRelationship | Set-OrganizationRelationship -TargetOwaURL
https://mail.cp.com/owa

You need to reconfigure the profile in the mobile device. I changed the servername in my IPhone 6.

OWA

OWA for Office 365 will prompt for redirection URL. Once you click on this link, you will be redirected to office365 OWA URL after verifying single sign on with ADFS. If you are accessing OWA from domain joined computer then you will not be asked for the password but if you are accessing OWA from a non-domain joined computer then you will be prompted for a password. Make sure to enter UPN and password in single sign-on.

ADFS login prompt came from non-domain joined computer.

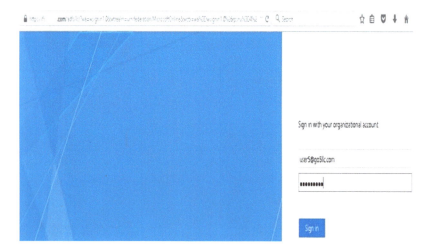

If you are using a domain joined then make sure to add your ADFS url in the internet options à Local intranet to bypass the ADFS login step. Once you have this configured then you will not see the above page or ADFS login popup.

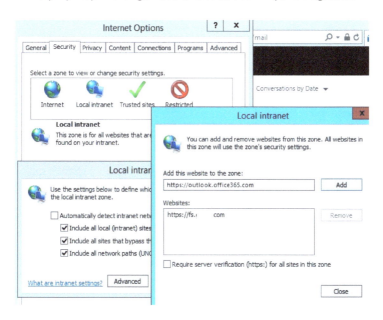

User5 finally logged in.

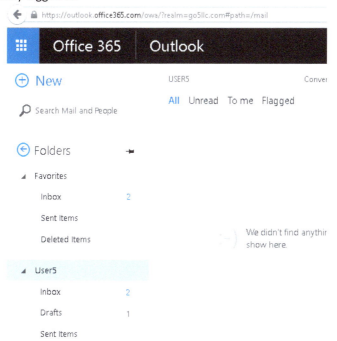

Make sure you login to the computer with the same domain login as OWA else ADFS will try to login with domain login user and fail if this user's account is not present in office 365.

Outlook Anywhere

Before Migration: Normal connection

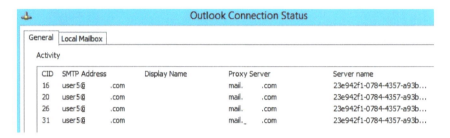

Now I am migrating the user to Office 365

You will get a popup to login. I would recommend to close outlook and reopen. Then provide a password when popup comes because you may still need to restart outlook after popup comes to restart outlook.

Now if we the connection status then we will see displayname will come up and Server name will show the Office 365 URL.

We also tested office 365 to Exchange 2013 mailbox migration and found. **You need to close and reopen outlook in both the migration.** The only difference is Exchange 2013 uses AD login so it will not prompt you for id and password but when you move a mailbox to office 365 then you need to provide login id(UPN) and password

Public Folders

Office 365 and Exchange 2013 support hosting public folders on the Exchange Online & migrating public folders. We can configure public folders so that users in either the on-premises or Exchange Online organization have access to public folders in either organization. Our main priority will be to remove legacy Public Folders. So keep the Public folders either in Exchange online or Exchange 2013. You can't coexist them.

To allow Exchange Online users to access public folders, run the below mention command in your office 365 PowerShell.

Set-OrganizationConfig -PublicFoldersEnabled Remote -RemotePublicFolderMailboxes PF-mailbox1,PF-mailbox2

You need to add all Public Folder mailboxes in RemotePublicFolderMailboxes which you can get from exchange management shell by running the below mentioned command:

Get-mailbox –PublicFolder

There is no native way of migrating Public Folder mailboxes from Exchange 2013 to Office 365. We need to check for the tool. Dell (Quest) Migration Manager for Exchange does not migrate it. So we are left with BitTitan's MigrationWiz and BinaryTree. I would prefer MigrationWiz which is a simple migration tool.

Calendar Sharing: Full or limited details:

If your org supports full details calendar sharing then you need to add sharing rule in the sharing policy for SMTP domain with max calendar access.

IRM

IRM is supported in the Office 365 so we can protect our emails and document. This needs a proper planning and I would recommend the MS KB jj659052 to be your link and document to follow for this.

Export & Import Retention Tag

Again for this please follow MS KB jj907307 as we can export and import retention tag.

Troubleshooting Hybrid:

Check out the following resources recommended by Microsoft to resolve some common hybrid deployment configuration issues:

- Troubleshoot a hybrid deployment – follow MS KB jj659053.
- "troubleshooting-migration-issues-in-exchange-hybrid-environment" in google for reading.
- Additionally you might be able to open a support ticket from office 365 Portal

ABOUT THE AUTHOR

Chetan is an accomplished migration specialist and a to-the-point technical author with various white papers and contributions to various technical sites. He has a Bachelor's in Computers (B.E.) and various MCSA, MCSA, MCTS, MCITP in Windows 2000, 2003, 2008 and 2012. His other expertise are in Exchange 2003, 2007, 2010, 2013, 2016, Skype for Business, Hybrid and Native Deployments, SAN, NAS and Redundant Clusters, Windows XP, 7 and 10 Clients, VMWare, Hyper-V and Cloud Computing.

He is also a certified CompTIA, HP and Dell Technician and has also been a Microsoft Certified Trainer (MCT) since August 2004 mainly concentrating on System and Infrastructure and masters infrastructure migrations complexities and global clustering and DAG setups.

www.ingramcontent.com/pod-product-compliance
Lightning Source LLC
Chambersburg PA
CBHW041149050326
40689CB00004B/713